How
to be a
Jewelry Detective

by C. Jeanenne Bell, G.G.

A Division of Antiques Detectives Inc.

Published by A.D. Publishing
7325 Quivira Rd. #238
Shawnee, Kansas 66216
Telephone: (913) 962-0085

Special thanks to:

Tom Besgrove - Graphic and Cover Design
Cheryll Jones - Cover Photos
Sally Bell Stites - Original Cover Layout
Lisa Bell Underwood - Assistant Editor

Gemological Institute of America - for allowing us to reprint illustrations from their course.

Sue Brown, Antique Jewelry, 1 Stoke 7, Davis Muse, London, for allowing me to photograph her jewelry.

Massada Antiques, Bond St. Antique Center, London, for allowing me to photograph their jewelry.

Frank Axelrod Antiques for allowing me to photograph his cameo.

Shirley Swabb for sharing a piece from her private collection.

Michael Marshall - my modern day "Watson".

ISBN: 0-9703378-0-9

Printed the the U.S.A.

Dedicated with love and gratitude to:

The One from Whom all good things cometh

and
my parents

Aaron Belton Noblittt
who had the soul of an artist and the hands of a jeweler

and

Anne Hooper Noblitt
who instilled in me a passion for solving mysteries

and
my husband & helpmate

Michael T. Marshall

TABLE OF CONTENTS

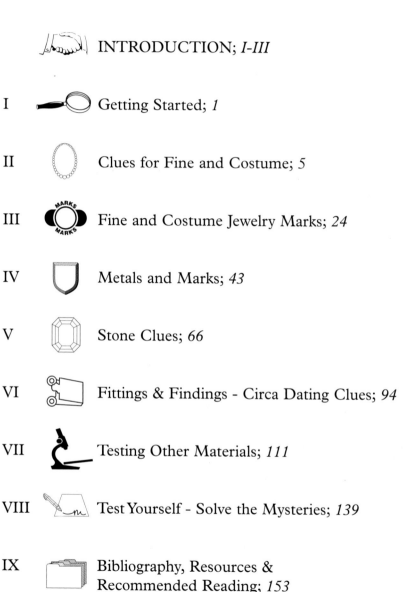

Introduction

Sherlock Holmes was a master of "deductive reasoning." With his seemingly instinctive glance at a room he could recite volumes about what had happened in the room, and about the people who lived there. In answer to Dr. Watson's inevitable look of amazement, Holmes' famous reply was always, "it is elementary my dear Watson, elementary".

A great deal of my time is spent traveling around the country doing seminars and presentations about antique jewelry. One of my favorite ways to end a presentation is to get items from the audience and do a "show and tell". The audience is usually amazed at what I can tell them about the age, history, material, and value of the piece after a brief examination.

When I examine a piece of jewelry I feel like Sherlock Holmes searching for clues. "What is it", "When was it made?", Is it fine or costume jewelry?", "Is it collectable?", and " Are the stones real?", are but a few of the questions that need an answer.

For years, my address has been listed in my book <u>Answers to Questions About Old Jewelry 1840-1950</u> and Tony Hymen's <u>Trash or Treasures</u>. As a result, I have received numerous calls and letters from people who want to sell their jewelry or people who have questions about jewelry that they have inherited.

Time after time I have gone through a litany of questions to help me determine what they had so that I could tell them about the piece from the information that they provided. Finally I decided to write a book about how to look for clues so that these people could gather them and determine what they had before they called.

Discovering these answers is like being a detective. First you gather the clues. Then you rule out the suspects, and hopefully solve the mystery. After thirty years, I still find this fun and exciting!

Whether you are a dealer, collector or just curious about jewelry, this book can help you solve the mysteries of jewelry. Because so much of what I've learned is elementary or basic, I can share it with you. Then you can put this information to use answering your questions about jewelry .

You will discover:

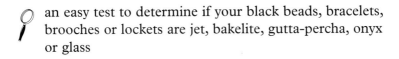 an easy test to determine if your black beads, bracelets, brooches or lockets are jet, bakelite, gutta-percha, onyx or glass

how to separate plastic from other plastic looking materials such as amber or tortoise shell

how to find clues that tell if a piece is costume jewelry set with fake stones or fine jewelry set with gemstones

what the marks and numbers inside a ring or on a brooch or pendant mean

what the terms gold, gold filled, gold plated, silver, silver plated and white metal tell about a piece

how the back of a piece can help you determine its age

how easy it is to use your basic tools–your eyes, ears, mouth, nose and hands–to help solve the mysteries

This book will help you explore the elements that are combined to make a piece of jewelry. These include metals, marks, stones, findings and other materials and embellishments. Most of the clues can be discovered using tools that you already have–your eyes, ears nose and teeth. The tests that make use of these tools will be explained later in detail and are easy to perform.

Don't forget to keep your "tools" in good condition by practicing their use as much as possible. Train your senses by going to as many antiques shows as possible. Let your eyes take in all the details of each piece. Hold it in your hand and note if it feels heavier or lighter than it looks. Over the years, I've had many strange looks when I rub a piece gently or tap it lightly against my teeth. Most people do not realize that I may be testing a pearl or listening for a sound that helps me determine what the material might be. Also use your mouth to ask questions. Knowledgeable dealers are always happy to share information about their jewelry.

Visit as many museums as possible. Look at the jewelry that the people are wearing in the portraits. Check out the date of the painting. The jewelry they are wearing is as old or older than that date.

Old photographs are also helpful. Notice how the pieces were worn. People usually wore their best jewelry for a photographic "sitting" and often this included jewelry that had been passed down in the family.

If this sounds like fun then you are a perfect candidate for the title of *JEWELRY DETECTIVE*. Not only is it fun but you may be surprised at how easy it becomes.

Ready? Let's begin!

Kate Hawkins Hooper, the author's Grandmother wearing dress clips, circa 1930's. They appear to be bakelite & shinestones and the set could have been sold with the dress or purchased separately.

Chapter I

Getting Started

Every good detective needs some basic tools. The first necessity is a magnifying glass. It doesn't have to be a big one like Sherlock Holmes uses, in fact two small ones will do just fine. In the jewelry trade these are called "loupes". Why two? Because although they both perform the function of making things easier to see, each is used for a different task.

Just looking!
(Photo by Cheryll Jones)

The cup loupe looks like a little cup without a handle. At the bottom is a magnifying glass. It is used by putting the large open end over your eye and then bringing the object up to the eye until it comes into focus. Sometimes it is as close as two inches. The power that I use is 2-1/2. This is excellent for reading the numbers, engravings and stampings on a piece of jewelry. Cup loupes are available for $6.50. *(See the order form in the back of this book.)*

The other loupe that I use has a 10X, fully corrected lens. This means that it magnifies the piece 10 times and it is fully corrected for depth distortion and color perception. Gemologist and appraisers use this type loupe to identify and grade gemstones.

This book is not intended to make you an appraiser but you do need this type of loupe to look at the outside and inside of a stone. It will help you determine whether you are looking at a man made material or a gemstone. A good, fully corrected loupe can be purchased for about $40.00. A beginners loupe (10X but not fully corrected) can be purchased for less than $20.00.

With these basic tools, plus my "built- ins", I am ready to start. I usually have a tray of jewelry from the audience and I start by picking up the closest one to my hand. First I take a cursory look at the item. I use my cup loupe to examine the front and back of the piece. With my 10X loupe I check out the stones. Next I appear to briefly put the piece in my mouth.

Now I am ready to tell the owner that the pin was made between 1890-1910 and it is Edwardian in style. It is made of gold over brass and embellished with "faux pearls" and a "glass stone". Retail value approximately $85.00

How did I come to this conclusion in just a few seconds? Let's examine what I really did when it appeared that I just "looked" at the piece.

The second that I picked up the piece my hands automatically noted the "heft" or weight of the piece. My fingers rubbed over the front and back of the piece to feel if the settings were smooth or rough. With my cup loupe I examined the detail and overall scale of the pin. Next, I noted the type of hinge and clasp assembly. The ball hinge and the C clasp, along with the scale and style of the piece helped me determine that it was from the Edwardian time period.

Next, I examined the edges for "wear". Here I noted brass showing along the edges of the piece that had received the most wear. This confirmed that the pin was gold over brass .

For examining the stone I used my 10X loupe. With it I was able to find a glass bubble inside the stone indicating that it was man made. This along with the abraded facet junctions lead me to conclude that the stone was glass.

Next, by rubbing the "pearls" gently across my teeth and feeling their smoothness, I concluded that they were not "real".

The pin had provided the clues. I knew how to look for them and add them together to find the right answers. If I were a fairly new **JEWELRY DETECTIVE**, I would have looked in a price guide for comparable pieces made of gold over brass and set with faux stones from the same time period. Then I could come up with a retail price ($85.00) or a range of retail values($75-95.00).

At a recent show a young lady came prepared with four zip-lock bags of jewelry. "It's probably all junk" she said " but I would like to know for sure". As I took a cursory look through the plastic I was about to agree with her, but suddenly my hand touched something that felt good. The minute that I lifted it out of the bag I was aware of the "heft"or weight of the brooch. As my fingers rubbed against the piece I noted that is was very well made. Even though it didn't have any markings I concluded by the "heft" that it was probably platinum. By the way that the stones were set I knew that they were probably diamonds.

Trying not to show my excitement, I calmly asked her where she had gotten it. "At a garage sale" she replied. "Do you remember what you paid for it", I asked. "Not more than a dollar", she replied, "that's my limit. It was probably in a box marked "your choice $1.00". It's not really my style but I thought that it was pretty so I bought it. I've never worn it, but my children have used it to play "dress-up".

After further examination, I asked her if she would like to be on national television and hear my appraisal. Treasures in Your Home (on the PAX network) set a date for the appraisal.

Prior to the show, the owner's curiosity lead to her asking if the brooch would bring enough money for her to take her children to Disney World. Not wanting to spoil the surprise, I told her it was according to whether she wanted to drive or fly. She informed me that she had already saved $1,000.00 for the trip. "In that case", I replied, "maybe the brooch will bring enough for your family to have a modest trip".

A few weeks later, I had the pleasure of telling her on national television that her $1.00 purchase was valued at between $8,000 and $10,000. She agreed to put the brooch on the <u>Treasures in Your Home</u> website. It sold for $9,000. To put it mildly, she was surprised and delighted!

What clues helped me separate this fine jewelry piece from the costume jewelry in the bag? Read on!

Jewelry Detective, Jeanenne Bell, TV Host John Burke and Treasure Finder Karen on the set of <u>Treasures In Your Home</u>.

Chapter II

Clues for Fine and Costume

In this chapter we will discover the clues used to separate fine jewelry from costume pieces. The term fine jewelry will be used to describe pieces made from precious metal and often embellished with natural or man made, synthetic stones. Synthetic stones are included because in the 1920's and 30's they were often used in the form of baguettes with the finest of natural stones.

As usual there are exceptions to every rule. During the Art Nouveau time period many famous designers such as Lalique used materials with little or no intrinsic value to make museum quality pieces. Also keep in mind that value is a "transient". Materials that have intrinsic value in one time period may be without this same value in another. For example, when aluminum was discovered in the mid-1800's, it was used for jewelry. It's rarity made it more valuable than gold. (Keep this in mind when you use your aluminum pans.) In the mid 1800's human hair was much more valuable than silver. Many beautiful pieces of jewelry were made from it. I have even written a book entitled <u>The Collectors Encyclopedia of Hair Work Jewelry</u>. Having stated all of these facts, we will use the general definition for fine jewelry in this chapter.

Fine jewelry is made to last and can be passed down from generation to generation. Costume or fashion jewelry as it is sometimes called is considered more temporary. Used to compliment prevailing fashions, it is usually made of base metals or plastics and embellished with imitation stones. If it happened to look real, so much the better!

Costume jewelry was often deliberately made to imitate fine jewelry so that it's owner could experience the pride of wearing an expensive looking piece even if they could not afford the real thing. At other times the designers embellished their pieces with such enormous "stones" that no one would ever mistake them for "real". Costume jewelry designers could also depart from fine jewelry styles to the fun and frivolous. Because much of this jewelry was inexpensive, if the customer tired of the piece, it could be discarded or retired without a great deal of regret.

Nineteenth century costume jewelry was made using base metals such as brass, copper, nickel silver, steel or even iron. The brass and copper pieces were usually electroplated with gold or silver. The jewelry was usually stamped or "die struck". For more information about these processes refer to <u>Answers to Questions About Old Jewelry (1840-1950), 5th Edition</u>, Jeanenne Bell.

The twentieth century brought the wide use of what is commonly referred to as "white metal". This mixture of tin, lead, bismuth, antimony and cadmium, has a low melting point and it is perfect for making large quantities of inexpensive jewelry.

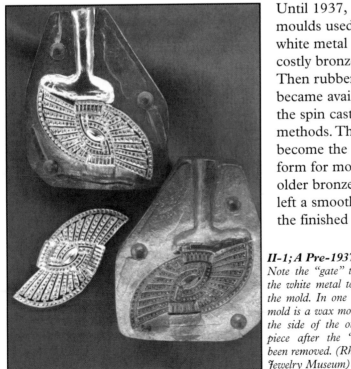

Until 1937, the moulds used to cast white metal were costly bronze ones. Then rubber moulds became available for the spin casting methods. They soon become the accepted form for moulds. The older bronze moulds left a smooth back on the finished piece.

II-1; A Pre-1937 Mold
Note the "gate" that allows the white metal to flow into the mold. In one side of the mold is a wax model and on the side of the other is the piece after the "gate" has been removed. (Rhode Island Jewelry Museum)

II-2; Cutting a rubber mold. (American Jewelry Products, Rhode Island)

DIAMOND CAPERS

A lady brought two very simular looking watch bands to a Home Show presentation that I did recently. She had purchased them at a thrift store for $10.00. I informed her that one was set with rhinestones but that that the other one was made of platinum and set with diamonds. Needless to say she was delighted to find out that it was valued at over $1,000.

At another show, a young lady brought in a wrist watch with a lid. It was covered with white brilliant stones that continued around the band. "I know that they are not diamonds", she said, "I would just like to know how old it is. I paid $35.00 for it at an auction because I thought it was pretty". After examining the watch, I asked her who had told her that they were not diamonds. "The auctioneer", she replied. You can imagine how her face lit up in surprise and awe when I told her that they were diamonds set in platinum with a retail value between $3,500.00 and $4,500.00.

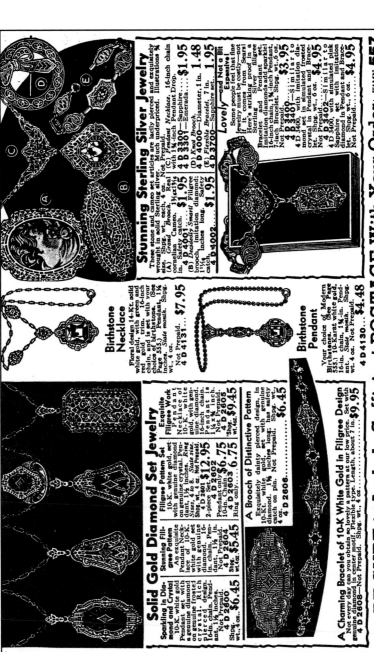

II-A; Filigree jewelry made of "solid gold" and others made of sterling silver. Many of the same "dies" were used for both materials. This ad appeared in the Sears & Roebuck catalog 1933-34.

THE CLUES

What do these two true stories have in common? In each episode both the buyers and the sellers did not know a simple way to tell if the piece was costume jewelry.

The picture below shows a pin watch, a brooch and a bracelet. Can you tell if any of the pieces have diamonds? Most people just guess and say that one piece has stones with more "sparkle" than the others but they are not always right. I have shown the actual pieces to dozens of people and not one of them bothered to turn the pieces over and look at the back. Often the back of a piece will offer more clues than the front.

Let's look at the backs of these three pieces. (See photo **#II-4**) Notice that the brooch has small openings behind each stone. The pin watch and bracelet have smooth backs without any openings. Diamonds set in the last 200 years would not be set this way. Diamonds need openings so that light can be reflected and refracted through the stone for maximum brilliance. The brooch has prongs holding the larger stones and tiny beads holding the small ones. (See photo **#II-5, 6**) Conclusion: the brooch could be a piece of fine jewelry. Finding a gold marking might verify this fact.

Now look again at the front of the other two pieces. Note that the pin watch has tiny beads sometimes used to hold diamonds in fine

II-3; *Which piece has the diamonds?*

jewelry. A closer look however will reveal that the beads are not touching or holding the stones in place. The stones are glued in. Rhinestones do not need the openings that diamonds do. In fact the closed back allows for a more secure gluing of the stones.

II-4

A closer look at the bracelet shows that the boat shaped stones (navette) are set in prongs but that the small stones are glued in. (See photo **#II-7,8**) Conclusion: these are both spin cast white metal that has been white gold electroplated and set with what is commonly called rhinestones.

This is probably as good a time as any to stress that a good detective gathers ALL of the clues and uses deductive reasoning BEFORE coming to any conclusion. For instance open backs only ___indicate___ a possibility of precious stones.

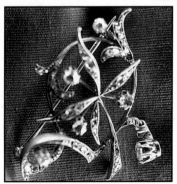 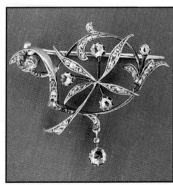

II-5,6; Note that the larger stones are set up in prongs; smaller ones are held in with gold beads.

II-7,8; The stones in the watch pin are set down into the white metal and glued. The small beads are not touching the stone. The navette stones in the bracelet are held by metal but the small stones are only glued.

FOILED AGAIN

Photograph number **#II-9** shows the back of a dress clip circa 1930-40's. The backs of the stones are open but notice that the stones are "foiled back". This is the gold colored backing that is so obvious in this photograph. Unfortunately, the backs of most foil back stones have darkened with age and dirt and are not this shiny. Sometimes the backing has been removed by improper cleaning. Consequently, it takes a close look with a loupe to discover traces of the foil backing.

II-9; The back of a dress clip with foiled "stones".

Some pieces will have openings behind the stones and do not have foil or traces of foil. What then? A good detective looks for other clues.

The prongs that secure the stones can offer more clues as to whether the piece is fine or costume jewelry. Photograph **#II-10** shows the prongs of a costume brooch and those of a gold ring. Notice how two dimensional and flat looking the prongs on the left (the costume piece) when compared to the gold ring on the right. "Heads" on fine jewelry pieces are usually made with round straight prongs and a notched out "seat" for the girdle of the stone. The stone is set and the prongs are bent over the stone and then filed off to fit the size of the stone. Notice how the prongs go straight up and then bend over the stone. This is a clue that the piece is fine jewelry. Remember these clues are indicators <u>not</u> conclusions. To find out more about what the stones might be refer to Chapter V for Stone Clues.

II-10; Note how flat the prongs are on this costume piece. They wrap over the stone.

II-10; The prongs on this 14k ring are round and straight until they reach the top of the stone. Then the prongs are bent over and filed off to provide a tip to hold the stone in place.

BACK TO BACK CLUES

The findings on the back of a piece often help to determine its age. Now that we know the pieces that are costume and the piece that is fine jewelry let's look to see what else we can find out about the brooch, pin watch and bracelet.

II-11; Fittings can be clues to circa dating.

The style and scale of the pin watch and bracelet lead one to believe that they could have been made in the 1920-30's. The brooch has the style and scale of an Edwardian piece from the turn of the century (1880-1900). These date can be confirmed by again looking at the back of the pieces. The pin watch has a ball joint (see under "findings") that was used from the 1890's onward. The type of safety clasp on the pin was not available until the 1920's. The date of 1920-30's is probably the correct conclusion for the pin watch.

The brooch has a tube hinge and a "C" clasp which is an earlier combination. Again, these clues back up my theory.

A good detective will continue to search for clues by checking the piece under magnification to see if there are any metal markings or maker's marks. The chapter on metal and markings will help you decipher them.

II-12; JBA Trademark.

The bracelet however, could be a surprise. It has a trademark which is the company mark for this author's line of revival jewelry. Knowing this mark one could conclude that it is <u>new</u>. Refer to the list of maker's marks in Chapter III.

Remember that a piece made of spin cast white metal will be thicker than its fine jewelry counterpart. Because white metal is softer it needs to be thicker than a gold item. Also notice that even though the pieces are thicker the "heft" is still light for its size.

A 'HEFTY" CLUE

Heft is always an important clue for the jewelry detective. Always be conscience of the weight of a piece the minute you pick it up. If the people involved in the following true story had known the secret of "heft" it would have saved them a lot of postage and insurance.

A few months ago a lady in another state telephoned to tell me that she desperately needed an appraisal on a necklace she had inherited. She had taken it to her local jeweler and he had told her that he could not appraise it because is was so old and rare. The

II-13; Coral colored rose bead alternating with green faceted balls and gold colored beads.

II-14; *Note the straight mold line running from the top to the bottom of the bead.*

description of the necklace indicated that it could be made up of carved coral roses. I promised her that I would appraise it.

When the package arrived it was tightly wrapped and heavily insured. Excitedly I opened the box. As I lifted the necklace I knew instantly that it was not coral. It was too lite. A brief look detected mould marks on each bead. They were plastic! The necklace was from about 1915-20's and approximately 40 inches long. It was very attractive but unfortunately not valuable enough to warrant an appraisal. You can imagine how disappointed she was with my findings.

A "TEETH" TEST FOR PEARLS

Most everyone has a strand of "pearls" from someone in their family. Often you can find "pearl" necklaces and pins in flea markets and thrift stores. Fortunately, separating fake pearls from cultured ones is a fairly easy mystery to solve. The test is so easy that you can become an expert in a short time.

For this test we will use another of our built-in tools. So far we have made use of our eyes and our hands (heft). Now its time to use our teeth. The only catch is that they have to be your REAL teeth.

Take one of the larger pearls in your hand and rub it gently across the outside of your front teeth. If it feels smooth it is a fake pearl. Cultured and natural pearls feel gritty or slightly sandy rough.

Now you know how to tell faux pearls from cultured. Unfortunately there isn't an easy way to tell if the pearls are cultured or <u>natural</u>. For this an x-ray machine is needed. To certify pearls as natural it is best to send them to a Gem Trade Laboratory such as the Gemological Institute of America. They will test them & provide a certificate as to their origin.

Remember that the faux pearl was invented between 1675 - 1700. Do not assume that just because a "pearl" necklace is old that it is real. As late as the 1930's, pearl advertising was so misleading that many men purchased what they thought were real pearls and presented them as wedding gifts to their brides. These were often treasured and passed down in the family.

II-B; Advertisement for "Betrothal" pearls from the Sears and Roebuck catalogue 1933-34. Believe it or not, these are "faux" pearls.

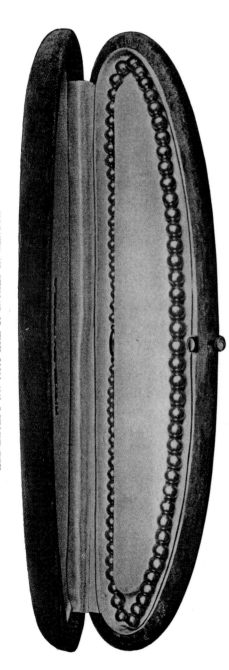

Pearl Neck Chains

ALL EXCEPT No. 70075 ARE 16 INCHES IN LENGTH

THE "RICHELIEU" PEARLS.

70060—Extra quality fine lustrous indestructible pearls; cream tinted; 10k solid gold clasp. These are perfectly matched and graduated and of a very fine color. Complete as shown with finest quality blue silk velvet oval box, white velvet lined. Cut is shown full size...**Each 36.00**

16
John·V·Farwell Company
CHICAGO

II-C; This advertisement from a 1917 John V. Farwell Co. catalog is for man made faux pearls but it's hard to determine this by reading the copy.

Unfortunately I've had the unpleasant obligation of informing many people that their grandmother's wedding pearls were imitation. This author will never forget that lady who took the news with relief instead of sadness. "Great" she responded. "Now I can wear them and enjoy them. Before, I was afraid to wear them because I thought that they were so valuable. They still have as much sentimental value to me as ever, but now I can wear them and enjoy them."

THE "EYES" HAVE IT!

Everyone knows the important part our eyes play when gathering clues about jewelry. It's very important to look at the size, scale, and workmanship but it's even more important to really "see" the piece. We are all guilty of "looking" but not really "seeing".

II-15; White metal rhinestone convertible brooch. c.1930's

Both costume and fine jewelry can often be surprising. Always be curious about hinges in unusual places, funny-looking backs, and other unusual details or 'fittings". If a dealer at a local antiques show had been more alert she would have noticed something different about the back on the brooch in photo **#II-15**. As you can see in photos **#II-16** and *17* it is a "duette"style set. The funny-looking mechanism enables the two sides of the brooch to be separated and worn as dress-clips or on a hat or a belt. Its value is approximately $350.00. The dealer sold it for $20.00.

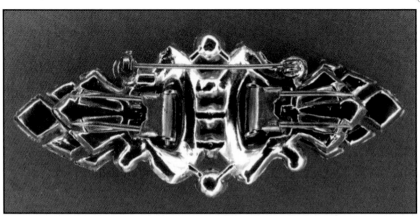

II-16; The back of photo II-15 showing the findings for a brooch or clips.

II-17; The piece converted into a brooch-clip combination.

The brooch in photo **#II-18 & 21** looks as if it might have a price of approximately $75.00. But by turning it over I'm sure that you will now know that it is a "duette" style brooch. Coro had trademarked the name "duette" so only pieces caring their trademark can officially be referred to as "Duette" sets. This set does not bear any marks.

Fine jewelry was also made in this style. In fact, many costume pieces were based on diamond and platinum originals. Rich or

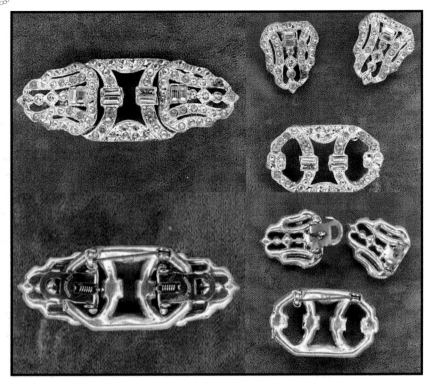

II-18-21; Another duette style brooch.

poor , it's always easier to rationalize buying a piece of jewelry that can serve more than one purpose. In the late nineteenth century tiaras were popular. Their pieces could be disconnected and special fittings could be attached by the owner to convert them into brooches, necklaces and hair ornaments. Convertible jewelry dates back to the Egyptians and even the Romans loved "flip" rings.

The ring in photo *#II-22* is 14K yellow gold and set with onyx. The 1942 date was probably the year of it's original owner's graduation. This could be a detriment for a new owner unless that year happened to be significant in their life. Consequently, it doesn't have a lot of "curb appeal", as it is referred to in the trade. A $250 price would reflect this.

II-22; One side of the flip ring.

By looking underneath the onyx center the surprise feature of a cameo is visible. A savvy Jewelry Detective will then look at the top, bottom and sides of the onyx mounting to discover whether the plaque flips from the top to the bottom or from the right to the left. As a "flip" ring the piece will sell for between $600 and $800.

II-23; The flip side.

Another "flip" ring (see photo *#II-24*) set with onyx. This one is centered with a small diamond. As it is flipped over (see photos *#II-25* and *26*) a beautiful shell cameo is revealed. This 18K white gold filigree ring (c.1920's-30's) sold for $995.00.

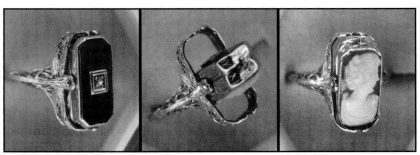

II-24; A white gold flip ring.   *II-25*   *II-26; The change is completed.*

As a Jewelry Detective expect to find the unexpected. Treat every piece as a suspect. The late Victorian brooch in photo *#II-27* looks very unsuspicious. Circa 1880's, it is made of gold over brass and set with a man-made "gold stone". It is pretty but ordinary - UNLESS you try unscrewing the ball knobs on each side. One side is immovable but the other side unscrews. Inside is a mini sewing kit, always ready to tackle those unexpected emergencies. It is complete with a needle, thread and a couple of pins.

Discoveries such as this can be found in all types of jewelry. Watch keys can sometimes be found <u>inside</u> the T-bar on an old watch chain. Look closely for side hinges on signet rings from the 1890-1910 time period. The engravable top plaque might open to reveal a locket. I own a bangle bracelet from the 1940's that has a lovely

II-27; Victorian brooch. It looks very ordinary to the unknowing eye. But by unscrewing the ball on the left side the Jewelry Detective will discover its secret compartment.

rhinestone clad central plaque that can be removed and worn as a brooch. I've even seen a stack-ring that could unfold and be used as a bangle bracelet. Convertible or multi-purpose jewelry is always a delightful "find". Remember don't just "look" at a piece,... really "see" it.

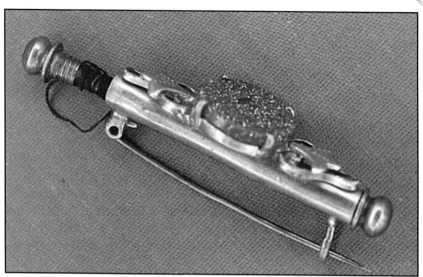

II-28; *The mysterious hiding place.*

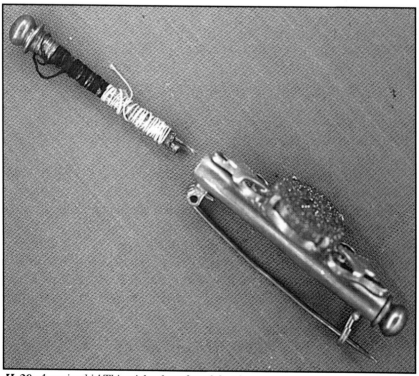

II-29; *A sewing kit! This triples the value of the piece.*

Chapter III

Fine and Costume Jewelry Marks
Retailers, Designers, Jewelers & Manufacturers Fine Jewelry Marks

Many designers, makers and retailers' names and marks can make a tremendous difference in the value and collectability of a piece. A collectible mark will often make a piece worth many times more than its intrinsic value. Pieces bearing names such as Tiffany, Cartier, and Van Cleef and Arpell will fetch 1-1/2 to 2 times their intrinsic value. Faberge pieces will command many times over the value of their stones and materials.

Costume jewelry has become so collectible that as plentiful as it is, the demand for some pieces often exceeds the supply. Consequently these pieces have become very expensive. It's hard to believe but some signed costume jewelry items that are made of base metal and set with glass can be sold for thousands of dollars. Of course if the pieces have provenance, as in the case of the costume jewelry in the "Jackie O" auction, the prices can be even more outrageous.

Other trade marks can provide information about when and where a piece was made or what the company manufactured. The following list contains these different types of marks.

A ★   **Allsop Bros.** - Corner Orchard and Camp Streets, Newark, NJ; 1894 - 1937; made gold and platinum rings; merged to form Allsop & Bliss in 1937.

 Arch Crown Mfg. Co. - Camp and Orchard Streets, Newark, NJ; 1904 - 1934; made diamond ring mountings.

Ostby and Barton Co. - 118 Richmond Street, Providence, RI; made rings from the 1800's - 1940's; a mark often encountered on all types of rings.

B. & B.

BATES & BACON

Bates & Bacon; Attlebora, MASS; made turn of the century "kant kum off" bangle bracelets "unique construction, with no visible joint or catch. Easy to put on or take off - Just a slight pull and a twist, yet it will not come unfastened when on the arm". Maker of gold and gold-filled items.

A. C. Becken Co.; Chicago, IL; 1934 jewelry wholesaler and distributor. This author has one of their 1886 catalogues in her collection.

Black, Starr & Frost - This retailer's roots go back to 1801. This name has been used since 1876. Famous prestigious American house; 1929 merged with Gorham Corp.

Boucheron - founded 1858 by Frenchman, Frederic Boucheron; lived 1830 - 1902; designers and retailers of luxury and medium priced jewelry

John Brogden - English goldsmith and jeweler; worked from 1842 - 1885; made prized archaeological style pieces with filigree and granulation.

Buccellati - founded 1919; jeweler and designer for the royal families of Spain, Egypt and Italy. Headquartered in Milan.

Bulgari - founded 1857; design styles based on classical and renaissance art with mosaic coloring. Often used ancient coins in their jewelry.

J.E. Caldwell & Co. - American retailer opened in 1830's. This name since 1848; 1992 the company was purchased by Carlyle & Co.

Cartier

Cartier; 1847 to present; world famous retailers and designers.

Castellani; 1814 to 1840; jeweler and designer using etruscan revival style.

Chaument & Cie - founded 1780; made wedding jewelry for Marie Louise in 1810; also known for sophisticated art deco pieces.

Child & Child - silversmiths and jewelers; London; 1880 - 1916.

COLONNA

(stamped)

Edward Colonna - jewelry designer in both the Art Nouveau and Art Deco styles. 1903 - 1905 worked in Samuel Bing's shop.

WLC

(in monogram)

Wilhelm Lucas van Cranch - 1861 - 1918; German painter and jeweler. Art Nouveau jewelry designer.

Etienne David - French jeweler; early 1900's; gold items and silver costume jewelry Art Deco style very collectable.

ФАБЕРЖЕ   **Faberge** - lived 1846 to 1920; famous Russian goldsmith and jeweler.

    Georges Fouquet - Art Deco; French jeweler and designer.

    Carlo Giuliano - worked 1867 - 1895; sons took over in 1895; closed 1914; renowned for beautiful enameled revival pieces.

    Jewelry Box Antiques - line of 18k reproduction jewelry and a line of costume jewelry since 1993.

La Cloche - founded 1875 - present; manufacturer and retailer known for Art Deco jewelry.

    Link & Angell; Newark, NJ; originally Link, Angell & Weiss; 1893 - 1915; Link & Angell 1915 - 1933.

    William Link, William Link Co.; Newark, NJ; 1871 - 1882; 1886 - 1923; made chains & bracelets.

R. LALIQUE
LALIQUE
R.L.   **Rene Jules Lalique**; lived 1860 - 1945; designer; jeweler; famous for Art Nouveau designs.

FROMENT MEURICE

(both father and son)   **Froment Meurice** - Francois Desere Froment - Meurice; Frenchman lived 1830 - 1867; Gothic Revival style and enamel Renaissance style; son, Emile Froment - Meurice; 1837 - 1913; Art Nouveau designs.

OP
(in a square monogram)

Otto Prutscher; 1880 - 1961; architect and jewelry designer; lightweight metals, beautiful enamel.

A.W.N. Pugin; Englishman lived 1812 - 1852; Gothic style and enamel pieces.

Riker Bros. - 42 Court Street, Newark, NJ; 1873 - 1940's; made beautiful gold, platinum and plique-a- jour enameled pieces.

Schepps - Seaman Schepps; American jewelry salon 1904 - 1929; reopened 1934; known for turbo shells mounted with gold wire and set with gemstones.

Starr - founded in New York in 1837 by Theodore B. Starr; purchased by Reed & Barton 1918; store closed in 1923.

Tiffany & Co. - founded United States; 1837 - present; famous retailer of upscale jewelry.

Louis Comfort Tiffany - 1848 - 1933; painter, interior designer, jewelry designer, glass maker and jeweler.

Van Cleef & Arpell - French company founded in 1906 - present; retailer and producer of fine jewelry.

Whiteside & Blank - Newark, NJ; 1899 - 1917; manufactured gold, platinum and plique-a-jour jewelry.

Philippe Wolfer - lived 1858 to 1929; jeweler who made wonderful use of nature's motifs.

J. R. Wood & Son, Inc.; New York, NY; ring manufacturer and wholesaler in the 1930's

Silver Marks

Silversmiths, Designers & Manufacturers

CRA
(pricked or scratched)

C. R. Ashbee; 1863 - 1942; leader of Arts & Crafts movement; founded school and guild of handicraft 1887 - 88; jewelry designer.

BGOH
(in a square)

Birmingham Guild of Handicraft; founded 1890; firm of craft jewelers; 1910 became part of Gittins Craftsman Ltd.

Elisabeth Bonte; French jeweler and designer famous for painted and engraved horn jewelry executed in the turn of the century styles.

BC

Bernard Cuzner; 1877 - 1956; English silversmith and jeweler; designed for Liberty & Co.

Theodore Fahrner; 1868 - 1928; German mass-produced jewelry manufacturer; low-carat gold or silver.

Piel Frères; company founded the mid 1800's; 1920 name changed to Paul Piel & Fils; worked with copper, silver and glass paste "stones" executed in the Art Nouveau style.

L. GAILLARD
(engraved)

Lucien Gaillard; born 1861; French silversmith, jeweler and enameler; opened workshop in 1900.

Authur & Georgie Gaskin; Birmingham, England; husband and wife; teachers, designers and illustrators; Arts and Crafts enamel pieces.

Gorham Co.; founded Gorham Corp., Inc.; Providence, RI; founded 1855; this mark was used in the late 19th and early 20th century; pieces were designed by artist; executed by silversmiths; made of silver gilt or copper. Note how they made this mark look like an English Hallmark.

Charles Horner; English designer and manufacturer; mostly silver with enamel.

George Jensen; lived 1866 - 1935; Danish goldsmith and silversmith; company still active today.

The Kalo Shop; founded in Chicago in 1900; handmade items in the Arts and Crafts style.

Wm. B. Kerr & Co.; Newark, NJ; founded 1855; mass produced pieces in the Neo-Renaissance style and the Art Nouveau style; company purchase by the Gorham Corp. in 1906.

Liberty & Co.; established in London in 1876; 1899 introduced "Cymric" line of jewelry by Arts & Crafts artists; manufactured by W. H. Haseler & Son in Birmingham.

Murrle, Bennett & Co.; German wholesaler and distributor 1884; very collectible mark.

PARTRIDGE **Fred I. Partridge**; English metal worker and jeweler; worked 1900 - 1908; designer; jeweler and wholesaler.

 Georges Pierre; French designer of handmade horn jewelry. Active late 1800's through the mid 1930's.

 Fritz Rossier; German manufacturer of silver jewelry in the Art Nouveau style.

EDWARD SPENCER DEL
(in a circle) **Edgar Simpson**; English designer; worked 1896 - 1910.

 Unger Bros.; in business 1879 - 1914; mass produced Art Nouveau jewelry 1904 - 1910.

 Wayne Silver Co.; founded 1895; manufacturer of silver jewelry.

Costume Jewelry Marks

Designers, Retailers & Manufacturers

 Anthony Novelty Co., Inc.; Providence, RI; trademark 1948

 Artistic Novelty Co., Inc.; New York; costume and precious stone jewelry; trademark 1920

 Associated Attleboro Mfg., Inc.; Attleboro, MA; trademark 1900 for expandable bracelet with heart or round locket center; very popular in the early 1900's.

 Avon Jewelry Mfg., Co., Inc.; Providence, RI; trademark 1962

 B. A. Ballou & Co., Inc.; Providence, RI; trademark used 1908 - 1950.

BALLOU   trademark 1919 - 1950's.

 trademark since 1947.

BEAU **Beaucraft Inc.**; Providence, RI; trademark 1947 - present.

BEAUCRAFT trademark 1947 - present.

 trademark 1947 - present.

B. A. Bliss Co.; founded 1875 - 1922 ;1893 started making silver jewelry; name changed to Napier in 1922 - present.

Fred A. Block; Chicago, IL; distributor of costume jewelry 1930's - 1950's; enameled costume jewelry with large stones.

A. Blumsteing, Inc.; New York, NY; trademark 1947 - present.

Jewels by Bogoff; Chicago, IL; founded by Henry Bogoff; (1940 - 1958).

Boucher, Marcel & Cie; New York; 1920's - 1971; manufacturer of quality costume jewelry; trademark 1940 - 1950's.

trademark late 1950's.

Hattie Carnegie, Inc.; New York; clothing designer with costume jewelry line; 1918 - 1970.

trademark 1919.

Hattie
Carnegie

Miss
Hattie

three of her trademarks

Gabrielle "Coco" Chanel; (1883 - 1971) clothing designer who designed her own line of costume jewelry; trademark 1914 - present.

trademark late 1950's

Cheever, Tweedy & Co., Inc.; North Attleboro, MA; trademark 1945; popular jewelry manufacturer 1940's - 50's.

CINER **Ciner Mfg. Co.**; New York, NY; trademark 1892 - present.

CINER trademark 1940.

 Ciro of Bond St., Inc.; New York, NY; trademark 1921 for watches.

Ciro trademark 1938 for jewelry

 C.I.S.; Countess Cissy Zoltowska; worked 1944 - 1951 in Lausanne; ceramic handmade costume jewelry.

Cohen & Rosenberger, Inc.; New York, NY; founded 1901; later changed to Coro, Inc.

Coro trademark 1939; between 1930 - 1960 this company used many different trademarks; most collectible are "Coro-Duette", patented 1930. The name "Coro" and Corocraft"

Coro DUETTE

Coro Craft Corocraft (highest priced line)

R DeROSA **Ralph De Rosa**; New York, 1935 - 1955; retro-modern styles with enameling and large stones; trademark 1940.

trademark 1946

Christian Dior; fashion designer; created 1947 "New Look"; designed his own line of costume jewelry; several manufacturers produced his jewelry; most pieces signed and dated.

Du Jay **Du Jay Co.**; New York, 1934 - 1947; rarely trademarked; small crystal rhinestones in pave' settings.

Eisenberg Original Dress Co.; founded 1914; began designing and manufacturing costume jewelry to go with clothes; quality silver and white metal costume jewelry 1930's - present. Eisenberg Original 1935 - 1945.

Eisenberg
ORIGINAL
trademark 1935 - 1940's on sterling

EISENBERG
ICE
Eisenberg Ice; trademark 1942 - 1958

 E; trademark 1942 - 1945

Eisenberg Ice **Eisenberg Ice**; trademark 1970 - present

"Priscilla" **Eisenstadt Mfg., Co.**; St. Louis, MO; trademark 1914; used all three marks through the 1940's.

PRISCILLA trademark 1916.

Priscilla trademark 1922.

Fashion Craft Jewelry Co., Inc.; New York; trademark 1942.

Fisher & Co.; Newark, NJ; trademark 1948

 Fishel, Nessler & Co.; New York; 1893 - 1937; manufacturer of sterling silver & rhinestone.

 Forstner Chain Corp.; Irvington, NJ; trademark 1937. popular mfg. in the 1940's-50's.

trademark 1962

Leo Glass & Co., Inc.; New York; factory established 1943 - 1957; classic motifs in silver and gold filled.

Miriam Haskell Jewels; founded 1924; 1930's established workshop to produce her designs; sold in the very finest stores; sold the company in the early 1950's; company still in business; early pieces unsigned; 1940's horseshoe shaped plate. Replaced by oval Mariam Haskell tag. Still used.

  Hobe' Cie Ltd.; New York, NY; 1903 - present; factory located in New York.

 Hollycraft, Corp.; in business from 1948 - 1965.

 Ideal Mfg.; Providence, RI; trademark 1921 - 1950 beautifully enameled silver jewelry.

Joseff - Hollywood; California; Eugene Joseff, jewelry designer for the film industry; 1938 - present; trademark 1938.

 trademark 1940.

 Dan Kasoff, Inc.; New York; 1956 - 1965; trademark 1956.

CLEO **Klein & Mueller, Inc.**; New York; trademark 1959.

 Kollmar & Jourdan; Germany; 1885 - 1977; gold-plated metal jewelry; trademark 1925.

KRAMER **Kramer Jewelry Creations, Inc.**; New York; 1943 - 1980; trademark 1943.
 trademark 1963.

KREMENTZ **Krementz & Co.**; Newark, NJ; 1884 - present; trademark 1884; rolled-gold plate jewelry.
 trademark 1884

 trademark 1930

 trademark - current mark

 Kenneth J. Lane; New York City; 1963 - present.

K.J.L. KJL

 Lester & Co.; Newark, NJ; trademark 1934.

 **D. Lisner & Co.**, Inc., New York; 1938 - present; trademark 1938.

trademark 1959.

MARATHON **Marathon Co.**; Attleboro, MASS; trademark 1914

trademark 1914 - 1950's

MATISSE **Matisse Ltd.**; Los Angeles, CA; trademark 1952.

MAZER **Mazer Bros.**; New York City; 1926 - 1951; started making costume jewelry in 1939.

JOMAZ **Joseph Mazer**; New York; 1946 - 1980; separated from his brother, Louis Mazer; trademark 1950's.

Iradj Moini; jewelry designer; went on his own in the late 1980's - present; makes use of brass and copper; no two pieces alike; time consuming handmade process; collectable contemporary designer.

MONET **Monet Mfg.**; founded by Michael & Jay Chernow; 1937 to present; Providence, RI; developed adjustable ear clip.

 Napier Co.; Meriden, CONN; 1922 - present; manufacturer of costume jewelry; trademark 1922.

trademark 1946

Panetta; New York City; 1945 - present; Italian immigrated to the U.S.; fine jeweler started making white metal costume jewelry during the depression; every piece signed.

Pennino **Frank A. J. Pennino; Pennino Bros.**; 1930 - 1961; New York; stamped and cast gold plated jewelry.

PERUZZI   BOSTON **Peruzzi Jewel Shop**; 1930's - 1981; Boston, MA; cast and stamped with mythological and archeological motifs.

P S CO **Plainville Stock Co.**; Plainville, MA; trademark 1884; also popular in the 1940's.

R ⹁ b a j ⹁ ⤴ **Francisco Rebages**; New York; 1932 - 1960; manufacturer; 1943 opened a retail shop; frequently used stamped copper.

Renee **Renee Novelties, Inc.**; Woodmere, NY; trademark 1934.

R É J A   **Réja**; New York; 1940 - 1954; trademark 1940.

{{ Réja }}   trademark 1940

Artistry in Jewels by Réja   trademark 1940

MATISSE
○ RENOR **Renoir of California, Inc.**; Los Angeles, CA; 1946 - 1964; popular for jewelry made of copper. Matisse Renoir - manufactured Matisse 1952 - 1964

House of Rousseau, Ltd.; New York, NY; trademark 1951.

SANDOR **Sandor Co.**; New York; 1940 - 1970; gold plated metals with cold-enameling.

Schiaparelli **Schiaparelli**; fashion designer; Elsa Schiaparelli (1890 - 1973); launched her own costume jewelry line; it has been described as "playful and zany"; artist such as Salvador Dali' sometimes designed for her.

 Schreiner; New York; 1944 - 1977; very collectible name in quality made costume jewelry.

Adele Simpson **Adele Simpson**; New York; designer who made use of classic motifs; trademark 1950's.

STARET **Staret**; Chicago, IL; 1941 - 1947; this company probably was inspired by the success of Eisenberg.

TRIFARI

KTF. **Trifari, Krussman & Fishel**; 1920 - present; many different trademarks, but most incorporate Trifari with a crown over the T. Designers of the "Jelly Belly" series of animals with lucite centers.

 Van Dell Co.; Providence, RI; popular name in costume jewelry during the 1940's - 50's; trademark 1939.

Weiss **Albert Weiss & Co., Inc.**; New York, NY; 1942 - 1971; trademark 1951.

Albert Weiss trademark 1951 in honor of the company President.

 **Whiting & Davis Chain Co.**; founded 1876 - present; worlds largest manufacturer of mesh products.

Collectible Mexican Jewelry Marks

A list of collectible marks would not be complete without including the names of some of the famous designers and manufacturers. They have become very popular with collectors.

   Hector Aguilar; Designer. Lived 1905 - 1986; worked 1930 - 1965.

 Los Castillo; Shop 1939 - present.

 Fred Davis; American lived 1880 - 1961; worked 1925 - 1960; designs inspired by pre-Columbian art; very collectible.

 Damaso Gallegos; Mexican born 1890 -

 Enrique Ledesma; Shop open until 1979.

 Margot; Woman artist and designer; Opened 1948.

 Antonio Peneda; Lived 1919 - 1985; Shop opened 1941; trademark 1950 - 1985 .

 **Isidor Garcia Pina**; Trademark 1950; The shop Maricela named after his daughter. Used .950 silver.

 Piedra y Plata; shop opened 1950; owned by Felipe Martinez.

 Salvador; 1952 Opened shop.

 Sigi; shop named La Mina opened 1953.

William Spratling; American; lived 1900 - 1967; trademark 1931 - 1945; often used .980 silver. Very collectible mark.

Chapter IV

Metals & Marks

It's very important to know the metal content of a piece of jewelry. This fact can determine whether or not a piece is costume or fine jewelry. The type of metal and the marks often found on it can have an enormous effect on value. Marks on the metal can provide clues as to where a piece was made, when it was made, who made it and what the metal might be.

At an antique show I purchased a watch chain that the dealer said was gold filled. When I got it home, a closer look with my cup loupe revealed an Eagle's head, which is the French mark for 18k gold. I had actually purchased a 48"long, 18k gold slide chain for only $35.00. Obviously, the dealer did not know what the Eagle's head signified.

This chapter will explore the types of metals most commonly used in jewelry and what the marks on these metals can tell us. Knowledge is power and sometimes that power equates to great buys!

Metals

PLATINUM

Platinum is a heavy, dense, hard metal. It is white in color with a slightly greyish cast. Although it was discovered in the 16th century it was used very little until the late 1800's. At that time a new torch was invented and it was hot enough that the average jeweler could work this dense metal. By 1900 it was very popular and continued to be so through-out the 1930's. Around 1915, 18K white gold was introduced as "a perfect imitation of the more expensive metal."

During world war II, platinum was restricted for use as catalyst in munitions plants. In the 1990's this beautiful metal made a strong come-back. Today it is once again recognized as a very valuable and popular metal.

Not only is platinum more expensive than gold, but an identical piece of jewelry made of gold would weigh a lot less. Also, 18K gold is only 75% gold and 25% base metal, where as a piece of platinum jewelry is usually 100 % platinum or 90% platinum and 10% iridium (which is also in the platinum metals group).

Platinum, iridium, palladium, rhodium, ruthenium and osmiridium are the metals that make up what is referred to as the platinum group. A combination of 90% platinum and 10% iridium is often used in jewelry.

MARKS:
    plat
    plat 10% irid
    platinum
    950

 used on pieces made in France since 1912.

 British platinum mark since 1973, when a mark for this metal became compulsory.

 Italian mark for Platinum

   Swiss mark used on watches

Note: some Mexican silver jewelry will be marked **950** designating silver content. These pieces usually have a maker's mark from Mexico.

RHODIUM

This is one of the six metals in the platinum group of metals.
It is a very hard metal and because of this it is used to plate
(electroplate) other metals to keep their shiny finish. The metals
most often plated with rhodium are sterling silver and stainless
steel.

MARKS:
    SS Rh (sterling silver rhodium finish)
    Stainless Rh (stainless steel rhodium finish)
    Rh (Rhodium)

GOLD

Gold comes out of the ground yellow and soft. In fact, in it's
purest form (24k) it is too soft to be suitable for most jewelry.
Consequently, other metals such as silver, nickel, zinc, and copper
are added to the pure gold to make it harder. The percentage of
these other metals determine the karat (K) of the gold. 18k gold is
made up of 750 parts of gold and 250 parts of other metals. The
color of these added metals determine the color of the gold. For
instance, pink gold is made by adding a mixture of silver, zinc and
copper. The depth of the pink color is determined by the amount
of copper used. White gold is a mixture of gold, nickel and zinc.

U.S. GOLD MARKS
18k	**.750**
14k	**.585**
10k	

BRITISH GOLD MARKS
22ct	**.916**
18ct	**.750**
15ct	**.625**
12ct	**.500**
9 ct	**.375**

(This gold quality mark will
proceed these % numbers
when the piece is hallmarked.)

Please note that the British use ct (carat) instead of the k for
gold designation.

SOME EUROPEAN GOLD MARKS

 French mark for 18k

 Italian mark for 18k

 Russian mark for 18k

 Russian mark for 14k

 Swiss mark for 18k

 Swiss mark for 14k

Before the metals act was passed in 1906 many misleading marks were used. The following were marks used as trade marks in the late 1800's. As you can see, the buyer probably believed that these marks indicated gold content, when in fact this was the trade mark that this company used for gold filled rings.

18 ☒   14 ☒   18 ☾   14 ☾

14 ✲   18.✲   C&C

IV-A; Clark & Coombs Co. 162 Clifford St., Providence, RI

This ring from the late 1800's is marked "SOLID GOLD". It is actually heavy gold filled. There are still many of these in circulation.

IV-1

FINE SOLID GOLD SHELL RINGS

PLEASE READ CAREFULLY.

These rings are exactly as represented, and will do all we claim for them. By avoiding misrepresentation, we have succeeded in obtaining not only a national reputation, but a trade that extends around the world. The length of time that a ring will wear is something that no man knows, as it all depends upon the occupation of the wearer. A ring worn by a clerk at the ribbon counter will wear longer than one of the same quality worn by a bricklayer, but it is an indisputable fact that the better the quality the longer the article will wear, so instead of asking, "How long will it wear?" why not ask "What is the quality?" Our opinion as to how long the different qualities will wear may not be of great value, but it, at least, has the merit of being an honest opinion based on fifteen years' experience.

Gold Shell.

Our gold shell rings are made by drawing a tube of solid 14 karat gold over a rod of composition metal, this shell being of sufficient thickness to justify us in guaranteeing them to wear 5, 3, 2 and 1 years and to give as good satisfaction as a solid 14 karat gold ring for the length of time, and the price places them in the reach of those who cannot afford the best solid goods.

If You Do Not Exceed Our Guarantee There Will Be No Complaint.

No. 15100 14 karat, warranted to wear 5 years.
Each $0.30   Dozen $3.25

No. 15101 14 karat, warranted to wear 3 years.
Each $0.15   Dozen $1.65

No. 15102 Warranted to wear 2 years.
Each $0.12   Dozen $1.25

No. 15103 Warranted to wear 1 year.
Each $0.10   Dozen $1.00

No. 15104 14 karat, warranted to wear 5 years.
Each $0.40   Dozen $4.50

No. 15105 14 karat, warranted to wear 3 years.
Each $0.25   Dozen $2.85

No. 15106 Warranted to wear 2 years.
Each $0.20   Dozen $2.25

No. 15107 Warranted to wear 1 year.
Each $0.15   Dozen $1.50

No. 15108 14 karat, warranted to wear 5 years.
Each $0.65   Dozen $7.00

No. 15109 14 karat, warranted to wear 3 years.
Each $0.40   Dozen $4.50

No. 15110 Warranted to wear 2 years.
Each $0.25   Dozen $2.75

No. 15111 Warranted to wear 1 year.
Each $0.20   Dozen $2.25

No. 15112 14 karat, warranted to wear 5 years.
Each $1.00   Dozen $11.00

No. 15113 14 karat, warranted to wear 3 years.
Each $0.50   Dozen $5.50

No. 15114 Warranted to wear 2 years.
Each $0.30   Dozen $3.25

No. 15115 Warranted to wear 1 year.
Each $0.25   Dozen $2.75

No. 15116 14 karat, warranted to wear 5 years.
Each $1.25   Dozen $14.00

No. 15117 14 karat, warranted to wear 3 years.
Each $0.75   Dozen $8.00

No. 15118 Warranted to wear 2 years.
Each $0.40   Dozen $4.50

No. 15119 Warranted to wear 1 year.
Each $0.30   Dozen $3.25

IV-B; Note the mark inside the ring on the upper right hand side of the page. Any one receiving this ring as a gift would assume it was 18k gold. Remember, "If you do not exceed our guarantee there will be no complaint". Every time I read this I can't help but laugh. Advertisement c.1898. These rings are all gold filled.

PLUMB GOLD

In the United States a piece designated as a certain karat gold can legally vary one half of a karat. As you might imagine, when a manufacturer has a choice he might use 13-1/2k instead of 14k. In 1978 the karat mark followed by a P was introduced so that a manufacturer could insure that a piece was "plumb" gold. If a piece is stamped 14kp it is guranteed by the manufacturer to be no less than 14k. As you can see, it is very important to know metal marks. Some people might mistake this mark for 14k gold plate.

GOLD FILLED

Gold filled is a confusing term. It's name implies that it is filled with gold. Not true!

It's easier to think of gold filled as a sandwich made up of a sheet of gold, a sheet of base metal, and another sheet of gold. The piece of jewelry is made from this sandwich and the metal touching your skin is gold but it has the added strength of the base metal. Some-times the piece will be made with only a gold top and a sheet of base metal.

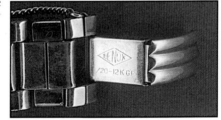

MARKS:
1/20 12KG.F.

IV-2; Gold Filled mark on a bracelet clasp.

The above mark means that 1/5th of the entire weight of the piece is 12k gold.

> **1/20 12kg.f on ss**
> **1/20 12k on sterling**
> **G.F.on S.S.**

These marks were used in 1942-45 when base metals were not available and sterling silver was substituted.

NOTE: Not all gold filled items are marked with these designations. Many 19th century American pocket watch case companies had their own way of describing the thickness of the outer layers of the sandwich. Look on the back cover and the dust cover for the words "Guaranteed 20 years". The cases were guaranteed for 10, 15, 20, and 25 years according to the thickness of the gold sheets. All watch cases guaranteed for these years are gold filled even if the 14k stamp precedes this guarantee.

ROLLED GOLD PLATE

This is an older term for gold filled. It is the same process but often the sheets of gold were thicker. The term was used in the 19th and early 20th century.

MARKS:
Rolled Gold
1/10 RGP
14KRGP (means that the piece is 14K rolled gold plate)

GOLD PLATED

This term sounds as if the piece should have a gold "plate" or sheet of gold over the item. Instead the entire piece is made of a base metal and then a very thin coating of gold is applied. This electroplating process was first used in the 1840's. Consequently, some very old electroplated pieces can be found. New costume jewelry is also gold electroplated.

Gold plated pieces can often be detected by a close examination of the places that get the most wear. Because the coating of gold is thin, wear points are usually easy to detect on old pieces.

IV-3; The tell-tale signs of a gold plated piece (also known as gold over brass).

Fine Electro Gold Plated Rings.

These rings do not have any Time Guarantee, but are the Finest on the Market for the Money.
(Sold only in Dozen and Gross Lots.—Assorted Sizes.)

No. 15214
Doz............$0.20
Gross......... 2.25

No. 15215
Doz............$0.30
Gross... .... 3.25

No. 15216
Doz............$0.40
Gross 4.00

No. 15217
Doz...........$0.75
Gross 7.50

No. 15218
Doz............$0.85
Gross......... 9.00

No. 15219
Doz...........$0.85
Gross......... 9.00

IV-C; The bands on the upper right hand side is detailed to show the marks. These rings are just gold electroplated. They are not guaranteed to wear for any length of time because the manufacturer knows that in a matter of days the base metal might show through.

MARKS:

14K H.G.E
18K H.G.E.

These marks are usually found on rings and many people mistake them for karat gold marks. Most pieces of electroplated jewelry are not marked. H.G.E. actually stands for "heavy gold electroplate".

SILVER

Silver has always been a popular metal. It's beautiful, feels good against the skin, wears well, and it's plentiful supply makes it is much less expensive than gold. Pure silver (.999 pure) is usually mixed with a base metal to make it more durable for jewelry.

STERLING SILVER

When refined silver is mixed with copper to be .925 fine it meets the requirements to be called "sterling". For hundreds of years, it's use and purity has been regulated. Great Britain began hallmarking silver over 700 years ago.

MARKS:
ster.
sterling
925

 English hallmark for sterling.

 French picion for sterling.

 Russian mark for 875 silver which is lower than our 925 standard for sterling.

 Russian silver mark for 916.6 purity.

 Russian silver mark for 947.9 purity which is higher than our sterling standard.

COIN SILVER

Coin silver was once the purity (.900) standard for coins. It was changed because so many silversmiths were melting the coins to make jewelry and watch cases. The name coin silver has continued to remain synonymous with .900 silver.

MARKS:
coin silver
900

800 SILVER

Another mark often encountered on pieces of jewelry consists of only the numbers 800. It means exactly what it indicates. The piece is made of 800 parts refined silver and approximately 200 parts base metal. It obviously contains less silver than coin silver or sterling. Pieces made in Germany often bear this mark. During the 1930's and 40's, many Italian cameo's were set in 800 silver.

MARK:
 800

SILVERPLATE

This is the same process used for gold electroplating. A thin coating of silver is applied to an item made of base metal by means of an electrical current. Nickel silver and copper are the most popular base metals used for silver plating.

MARKS:
 silverplate
 quadruple plate
 E.P.N.S (electro- plated nickel silver)

GERMAN SILVER

German silver is not German and it is not silver. This mixture of zinc, copper and nickel is called German because a German introduced it to England in the late 1700's. It had a silvery look so they named it German Silver. It is also known by the name "nickel silver".

MARKS:
 E.P.N.S. (electro-plated nickel silver)

VERMIEL

The French word vermiel is pronounced Vair-May and it means silver gilt. This old process of coating sterling silver with gold was very popular throughout the 1700's. In the 1800's it was discovered that mercury, which was used in the process, caused the workers to go blind and it was banned. Tiffany's revived and improved the process in 1956. They were able to achieve the glowing look without using the dangerous mercury.

MARKS:
> Gold items marked **925** or **sterling** are vermiel.

WHITE METALS

Some older costume jewelry is made of base metals such as copper, brass, german silver, iron and steel, but most 20th century pieces are made from what is commonly referred to as "white metal".

White metal is a mixture of tin, lead, bismuth, antimony and cadmium. The quality of the jewelry depends on the tin content which may vary from 17% to 92%. Many quality costume pieces have a tin content of 88%.

Because white metal has a low melting point it is almost impossible to repair. It tends to melt when touched by a torch even if the torch is in the hands of an expert jeweler. A substitute called JB Weld can sometimes be used for simple repairs.

METAL TESTING

Many jewelry pieces are not marked. Before 1906 karat marking was not compulsory. Some rings that were originally marked have lost their gold marks while being sized down. What is the new Jewelry Detective to do? How can we determine if a piece is gold? The first thing is to rule out other suspects. So begin by trying to determine if the piece is NOT gold. Use a loupe to examine the entire piece. Give particular attention to the areas that receive the most wear. If the piece has a dangle as in the case of the garnet necklace on page 49 (see photograph *#IV-3*) look closely at the edge of the piece that rubs against the chest.

Bracelets need to be checked all over with special attention given to clasps and other parts that might show wear. Look closely at chain links especially where they overlap each other. If they wear, this is usually the first area to show it. This change of color at the wear points is especially evident if the piece is gold or silver electroplated over brass or copper.

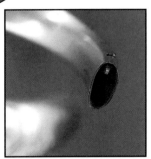

By looking closely at the hinged bangle in photograph number *#IV-4* you can see the shinny layer of gold and the layer of brass that make up the gold filled "sandwich". If wear points or gold sheets are visible then you can be positive that you do not have a piece of gold jewelry. You have narrowed down the suspects.

IV-4; This bangle bracelet is turned so that the light is reflecting off of the gold sheet. Reflected light can often be used to an advantage.

But what if there are not any wear points or visible layers? This means that further detection is necessary. A gold test can be done by a jeweler or gemologist for about $15.00. But if you are a dealer or collector, it might be less expensive in the long run to invest in some gold testing equipment.

Digital gold testers can be purchased for $100.00 to $600.00. I own one of the more expensive testers but my long time favorite way to test metals is the "acid test". A testing kit containing acid solutions for 18kt, 14kt, and 10kt can be purchased for approximately $45.00 at a jewelry supply company or use the order form in the back of this book. The kit is contained in a wooden box and comes complete with a touch stone. An extra touch stone can be purchased for about $4.00. Not included in the kit is the most important ingredient, nitric acid. This must be purchased at a chemical supply house. Needless to say it should be handled with care and stored in a glass or plastic container.

The first thing to do when acid testing is to prepare an area in which to test. I use a piece of formica covered with a white paper towel. Have a cup of soda water close at hand to neutralize any acid that might come in contact with your skin. Look for a place on the piece of jewelry to apply the acid. If the piece is monogramed or is deeply engraved, start

IV-B; Gold testing kit with 10k, 14k and 18k acid and a test stone.

by placing a drop of nitric acid in that area. If the nitric acid just lays there like a drop of clear water, the piece might possibly be gold. Next go to an area that may have gotten wear, such as the links of a chain. If on the engraved areas or wear points the acid starts forming tiny bubbles (effervescing) and turns green, it indicates gold over a brass base metal. If it effervesces and turns bluish the base metal is copper.

If the acid does not effervesce the piece is possibly gold. But how can we know for sure that it is not just a heavily gold-plated or gold filled piece? The only sure way is to file a mark deep enough to go past any gold sheets to the base metal. This notch must be made in an inconspicuous spot and be very small but deep. If there isn't a reaction when the acid is applied to the notch but the metal turns slightly darker, it is probably 10kt gold. If there isn't a reaction, and the acid stays clear, the piece is gold and higher than 10kt.

Now it is time to see what karat gold the piece really is. Take the piece of jewelry and by rubbing it across the touch stone make a mark approximately one inch long. Now put a drop of 14kt acid across the gold line on the stone. If the gold line dissolves, the piece is higher than 14kt. Next, try the 18kt solution on another area of the gold line. If it stays visible the piece it is at least 18kt gold. Then, try a 22kt gold acid solution and if the line disappears you can be sure that the piece is at least 18kt gold.

The mistake most people make when using a touch stone and acid solutions is that they do not file into the piece. If the piece is gold filled, a touch stone will indicate gold. You <u>must</u> <u>get</u> <u>past</u> the layer of gold for a true test. Some people are so afraid that they will damage the piece that gold filled or roll gold items are sometimes sold as gold. Again, use the thinnest, sharpest-edged testing file and always look for an inconspicuous spot to "nick". Then very carefully go deep enough to go past any layer of gold. My file marks are so tiny that it often takes a loupe to detect them. Never use a long file mark because this will not only damage the piece but it also greatly diminishes its' value.

TESTING PLATINUM

The heft of a platinum piece is usually a fairly accurate indication of the metal. To confirm this use a platinum solution and a touch stone. If the acid does not dissolve the mark on the touch stone the piece is platinum.

TESTING SILVER

To test silver begin by putting a drop of nitric acid on the back of a piece or on any monogrammed or engraved areas. This is often sufficient to detect the green or bluish colors of brass or copper base metals. If the piece is silver, nitric acid will turn the area a more whitish cloudy matte color. If the metal is coin silver the spot where the nitric was placed will turn blackish.

If the nitric acid does not give you definitive clues, a silver testing solution can be used. This is available at jewelers supply houses for about $4.00. The color that the solution turns when placed upon the area will determine the percentage of silver in the piece. If the piece is fine silver the solution should turn bright red. Sterling silver should turn dark red and 800 silver will turn brown.

WEIGHING METALS

Every good Jewelry Detective needs to to know how the weight of a piece of metal jewelry can effect its value and why.

Gold is sold by the ounce, the pennyweight (DWT), or the gram(GRM). An ounce of gold weighs 20 dwts (pennyweights) or 30 grams. It takes 1.5 grams to make one pennyweight. Consequently, when discount retailers of gold chain advertise their gold prices they always use "dollars per gram." The price looks less in grams than it would in pennyweights.

Gold has many "values". When gold is $300.00 an ounce, 14K casting grains used to make jewelry may be priced at $12.00 a dwt while the finished piece, which includes design and labor charges may be priced at $75.00 a dwt. At the same $300.00 per ounce, the piece of jewelry might "scrap" for less than $6.00 a dwt.

Platinum is more expensive than gold but it is also sold by the troy ounce. It is divided into the same measures of pennyweights or grams. Remember that it takes a smaller piece of platinum to weigh an ounce because it has a higher specific gravity. A good analogy of this is a 1" x 1" square of wood and a 1" x 1" square of steel. It would take a stack of the wooden cubes to weigh as much as one steel cube even though they are exactly the same size.

A platinum brooch will weigh (and consequently cost) more than a gold brooch cast from a wax from the same mould. Although their size will be identical, the platinum piece will weigh more and be more expensive.

My favorite way to weigh metals is with a scale that can be set to pennyweights or grams. There are many reliable models ranging in price from about ninety-five dollars to hundreds of dollars.

IV-C; This scale weighs pennyweights, grams and ounces. (See order form in the back of this book)

HALLMARKS

In the 14th century, England started a system to insure the quality of silver. These English hallmarks consist of an assay mark, a metal content mark, a letter date and sometimes a makers mark. These are usually "punched" into the metal. The shape of the punch containing these marks and the style of the letters are important in determining when a piece was made.

Town marks represent the city in which the piece was tested or "assayed" for metal content. Always start by determining this city and then proceed to the letter date.

The city assay marks are as follows:

 London

 Birmingham (when the anchor is upright it is on a silver piece. When it is on its side the piece is gold.)

 Chester

 Sheffield

Edinburg

 Glasgow

Letter dates are letters that correspond to the date that the piece was assayed. Not only must the style of the letter match up to a year but the shape of the box in which it is enclosed, must also match the example in the Hallmark Book.

Metal content marks can be as simple as 18ct or as mysterious as a lion passant for silver or a crown which signifies gold.

In 1854, 9ct, 12ct and 15ct gold was legalized in England. These do not have a crown but they do include carat marks and sometimes the carat value in decimals. In 1932, 12ct and 15ct gold were discontinued and 14ct became their new standard.

Fortunately there are many good hallmark books readily available at the libraries and book stores. One of my favorites is Bradbury's Book of Hallmarks. It is pocket sized and usually cost under $10.00.

French hallmarks are known as poicons. They are confusing and complicated as are many European ones. Some of these marks are listed under the appropriate metals at the beginning of this chapter. For a complete list of marks I recommend "Poicons d' Or et de Platine" by Tardy.

REGISTRY MARKS

Occasionally you will find a piece of jewelry with a British Registry mark. It is an interesting mark because it can tell you the date the piece was registered.

From 1842 through 1867 the mark has the shape of a diamond with a circle at the top. The circle should have the Roman Numeral I designating the piece is made of metal. After 1867 the circle was omitted and the information enclosed in the diamond was rearranged.

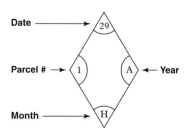

(Example from 1842 -1867)

Mark #1

Year →
Month →
Parcel # →
← Date

(Example from 1868 -1883)

Mark #2

Date →
Parcel # →
← Year
Month →

Both marks are the same month and day, April 29th. Mark number 1 was registered in the year 1861 and registry mark number 2 was dated 1871.

REGISTRY MONTH MARKS
1842-1883

January - C	July - I
February - G	August - R
March - W	September - D
April - H	October - B
May - E	November - K
June - M	December - A

YEAR OF REGISTRY MARKS
(diamond w/circle–Mark #1)
1842 - 1867

1842 - X	1855 - E
1843 - H	1856 - L
1844 - C	1857 - K
1845 - A	1858 - B
1846 - I	1859 - M
1847 - F	1860 - Z
1848 - U	1861 - R
1849 - S	1862 - O
1850 - V	1863 - G
1851 - P	1864 - N
1852 - D	1865 - W
1853 - Y	1866 - Q
1854 - J	1867 - T

YEAR OF REGISTRY MARKS
(diamond w/o circle– Mark #2)
1868-1883

1868 - X	1876 - V
1869 - G	1877 - P
1870 - C	1878 - D
1871 - A	1879 - Y
1872 - I	1880 - J
1873 - F	1881 - E
1874 - U	1882 - L
1875 - S	1883 - K

REGISTRY NUMBERS 1884-1980

In 1884 the diamond shape was replaced by the abbreviation $R^D N^O$ (Registry Number) followed by a number. Each year on the chart is followed by the first number issued in that year.

1 - 1884	447800 - 1905	718057 - 1926
20000 - 1885	471860 - 1906	726330 - 1927
40800 - 1886	493900 - 1907	734370 - 1928
64700 - 1887	518640 - 1908	742725 - 1929
91800 - 1888	535170 - 1909	751160 - 1930
117800 - 1889	552,000 - 1910	760583 - 1931
142300 - 1890	575817 - 1911	769670 - 1932
164000 - 1891	594195 - 1912	779292 - 1933
186400 - 1892	612431 - 1913	789019 - 1934
206100 - 1893	630190 - 1914	799097 - 1935
225000 - 1894	644935 - 1915	808794 - 1936
248200 - 1895	653521 - 1916	817293 - 1937
268800 - 1896	658988 - 1917	825231 - 1938
291400 - 1897	662872 - 1918	832610 - 1939
311677 - 1898	666128 - 1919	837520 - 1940
332200 - 1899	673750 - 1920	838590 - 1941
351600 - 1900	680147 - 1921	839230 - 1942
68186 - 1901	687144 - 1922	839980 - 1943
385180 - 1902	694999 - 1923	841040 - 1944
403200 - 1903	702671 - 1924	842670 - 1945
424400 - 1904	710165 - 1925	845550 - 1946

849730 - 1947	891665 - 1959	950046 - 1971
853260 - 1948	895000 - 1960	955342 - 1972
856999 - 1949	899914 - 1961	960708 - 1973
860854 - 1950	904638 - 1962	965185 - 1974
863970 - 1951	909364 - 1963	969249 - 1975
866280 - 1952	914536 - 1964	973838 - 1976
869300 - 1953	919607 - 1965	978426 - 1977
872531 - 1954	924510 - 1966	982815 - 1978
876067 - 1955	929335 - 1967	987910 - 1979
879282 - 1956	934515 - 1968	993012 - 1980
882949 - 1957	939875 - 1969	
887079 - 1958	944932 - 1970	

PATENT NUMBERS

The United States has issued patents since 1790. But the inventions were not numbered until 1836. Microsoft Encarta '96 defines a patent as "a document issued by the government conferring some special right or privilege. In the U.S. the term is now restricted principally to patents for inventions granted under federal statute. The specific attributes of novelty of the item for which a patent is sought are called claims. A patent gives the inventor the exclusive privilege of using a certain process or of making, using and selling a specific product or device for a specified period of time."

The patent numbers on a piece of jewelry refer to an invention such as a certain type clasp. Consequently, the patent date does not necessarily reflect the date that the piece was made. The patented feature could be used for years after its original patent date. Many pieces from the nineteenth century have the the actual patent date. *(see photo #IV-5)* The following list of numbers are the first patent issued in that year. (For instance, patent number 600,121 was issued in 1898.)

IV-5; Patent date of July 23, 1887 on a mesh bracelet.

PATENT NUMBERS
1836-1990

1 - 1836	146,124 - 1874	1,031,095 - 1912
110 - 1837	158,350 - 1875	1,049,326 - 1913
546 - 1838	171,641 - 1876	1,083,267 - 1914
1,061 - 1839	185,813 - 1877	1,123,212 - 1915
1,465 - 1840	198,733 - 1878	1,166,419 - 1916
1,923 - 1841	211,078 - 1879	1,210,389 - 1917
2,413 - 1842	223,211 - 1880	1,251,458 - 1918
2,901 - 1843	236,137 - 1881	1,290,027 - 1919
3,395 - 1844	251,685 - 1882	1,326,899 - 1920
3,873 - 1845	269,820 - 1883	1,364,063 - 1921
4,348 - 1846	291,016 - 1884	1,401,948 - 1922
4,914 - 1847	310,163 - 1885	1,440,362 - 1923
5,409 - 1848	333,494 - 1886	1,478,996 - 1924
5,993 - 1849	355,291 - 1887	1,521,590 - 1925
6,981 - 1850	375,172 - 1888	1,568,040 - 1926
7,875 - 1851	395,305 - 1889	1,612,700 - 1927
8,622 - 1852	418,665 - 1890	1,654,521 - 1928
9,512 - 1853	443,987 - 1891	1,696,897 - 1929
10,358 - 1854	466,315 - 1892	1,742,181 - 1930
12,117 - 1855	488,976 - 1893	1,787,424 - 1931
14,009 - 1856	511,744 - 1894	1,839,190 - 1932
16,324 - 1857	531,619 - 1895	1,892,663 - 1933
19,010 - 1858	552,502 - 1896	1,941,449 - 1934
22,477 - 1859	574,369 - 1897	1,985,878 - 1935
26,642 - 1860	596,467 - 1898	2,026,516 - 1936
31,005 - 1861	616,871 - 1899	2,066,309 - 1937
34,045 - 1862	640,167 - 1900	2,104,004 - 1938
37,266 - 1863	664,827 - 1901	2,141,080 - 1939
41,047 - 1864	690,385 - 1902	2,185,170 - 1940
45,685 - 1865	717,521 - 1903	2,227,418 - 1941
51,784 - 1866	748,567 - 1904	2,268,540 - 1942
60,658 - 1867	778,834 - 1905	2,307,007 - 1943
72,959 - 1868	808,618 - 1906	2,338,081 - 1944
85,503 - 1869	839,799 - 1907	2,366,154 - 1945
98,460 - 1870	875,679 - 1908	2,391,856 - 1946
110,617 - 1871	908,436 - 1909	2,413,675 - 1947
122,304 - 1872	945,010 - 1910	2,433,824 - 1948
134,504 - 1873	980,178 - 1911	2,457,797 - 1949

2,492,944 - 1950	3,163,865 - 1965	4,180,867 - 1980
2,535,016 - 1951	3,226,729 - 1966	4,242,717 - 1981
2,580,379 - 1952	3,295,143 - 1967	4,308,622 - 1982
2,624,046 - 1953	3,360,800 - 1968	4,336,579 - 1983
2,664,562 - 1954	3,419,907 - 1969	4,423,525 - 1984
2,698,434 - 1955	3,487,470 - 1970	4,490,885 - 1985
2,728,913 - 1956	3,551,909 - 1971	4,562,596 - 1986
2,775,762 - 1957	3,631,539 - 1972	4,633,526 - 1987
2,818,567 - 1958	3,707,729 - 1973	4,716,594 - 1988
2,866,973 - 1959	3,781,914 - 1974	4,794,652 - 1989
2,919,443 - 1960	3,858,241 - 1975	4,890,335 - 1990
2,966,681 - 1961	3,930,270 - 1976	
3,015,103 - 1962	4,000,520 - 1977	
3,070,801 - 1963	4,065,812 - 1978	
3,116,487 - 1964	4,131,952 - 1979	

PATENT MARKS:
Patented
Patent #
Ptnd.
PAT'D
Pat No

DESIGN NUMBERS

Jewelry detectives and collectors are always excited to find a piece with a Design Number. They can be a good clue as to when a piece was made and became popular. The following list has the year and the first Design Patent Number issued for that year.

1 - 1843	540 - 1853	1,703 - 1863
15 - 1844	626 - 1854	1,879 - 1864
27 - 1845	683 - 1855	2,018 - 1865
44 - 1846	753 - 1856	2,239 - 1866
103 - 1847	860 - 1857	2,533 - 1867
163 - 1848	973 - 1858	2,858 - 1868
209 - 1849	1,075 - 1859	3,304 - 1869
258 - 1850	1,183 - 1860	3,810 - 1870
341 - 1851	1,366 - 1861	4,547 - 1871
431 - 1852	1,508 - 1862	5,452 - 1872

DESIGN NUMBERS (cont.)

6,336 - 1873	43,073 - 1912	161,404 - 1951
7,083 - 1874	43,415 - 1913	165,568 - 1952
7,969 - 1875	45,098 - 1914	168,527 - 1953
8,884 - 1876	46,813 - 1915	171,241 - 1954
9,686 - 1877	48,358 - 1916	173,777 - 1955
10,384 - 1878	50,117 - 1917	176,490 - 1956
10,975 - 1879	51,629 - 1918	179,467 - 1957
11,567 - 1880	52,836 - 1919	181,829 - 1958
12,082 - 1881	54,359 - 1920	184,204 - 1959
12,647 - 1882	56,844 - 1921	186,973 - 1960
13,508 - 1883	60,121 - 1922	189,516 - 1961
14,528 - 1884	61,748 - 1923	192,004 - 1962
15,678 - 1885	63,675 - 1924	194,304 - 1963
16,451 - 1886	66,346 - 1925	197,269 - 1964
17,046 - 1887	69,170 - 1926	199,955 - 1965
17,995 - 1888	71,772 - 1927	203,379 - 1966
18,830 - 1889	74,159 - 1928	206,567 - 1967
19,533 - 1890	77,347 - 1929	209,732 - 1968
20,439 - 1891	80,254 - 1930	213,084 - 1969
21,275 - 1892	82,966 - 1931	216,419 - 1970
22,092 - 1893	85,903 - 1932	219,637 - 1971
22,994 - 1894	88,847 - 1933	222,793 - 1972
23,922 - 1895	91,258 - 1934	225,695 - 1973
25,037 - 1896	94,179 - 1935	229,729 - 1974
26,482 - 1897	98,045 - 1936	234,032 - 1975
28,113 - 1898	102,601 - 1937	238,315 - 1976
29,916 - 1899	107,738 - 1938	242,881 - 1977
32,055 - 1900	112,765 - 1939	246,811 - 1978
33,813 - 1901	118,358 - 1940	250,676 - 1979
35,547 - 1902	124,503 - 1941	253,796 - 1980
36,198 - 1903	130,989 - 1942	257,746 - 1981
36,723 - 1904	134,717 - 1943	262,495 - 1982
37,280 - 1905	136,946 - 1944	267,440 - 1983
37,766 - 1906	139,862 - 1945	272,009 - 1984
38,391 - 1907	143,386 - 1946	276,949 - 1985
38,980 - 1908	146,165 - 1947	282,020 - 1986
39,737 - 1909	148,267 - 1948	287,540 - 1987
40,424 - 1910	152,235 - 1949	293,500 - 1988
41,063 - 1911	156,686 - 1950	299,180 - 1989

MARKS:

Design #
Pat. D #

Can you discover the year that this design was first issued?

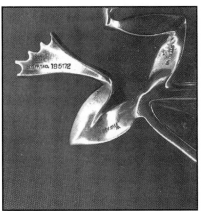

IV-5; *Design number 135,172 on a vermier "jelly belly" frog brooch.*

Chapter V

Stone Clues

Stones are often the most mysterious elements in jewelry. They not only add to the beauty of the piece but they can make a tremendous difference in value. Unfortunately, their mysteries are often the most difficult for the average Jewelry Detective to solve. The good news is that this chapter will offer clues to make this task easier.

In earlier chapters we discovered clues about metals, marks open backs and prongs that lead us to conclude what the stone might possibly be. In this chapter we will look for clues inside and outside the stones. Because this is not a course in gemology I can guarantee that you will not be a gemologist when you finish reading this chapter. If it does inspire this desire the Gemological Institute of America offers a home study course for these purposes. Their address and toll free number is listed in the Resource section of this book.

We will explore clues hidden inside the stone and tests that can help a lay person detect whether the stone is natural or man-made. Included are tests that can be done inexpensively in the home. We will also learn about some of the tools used by gemologists.

This chapter also explores the different cuts of stones and their evolution. The dates that certain cuts were invented or became popular can be a clue as to when it was "made". These same clues will rule out the years prior to the cuts introduction. If the piece contains a modern brilliant cut diamond it was most likely cut after the 1920's. If it is original to the piece, the jewelry is probably after that date also.

Before we begin to explore the mysteries of stones it is important to know some of the terms used.

NATURAL STONES are created by God inside the earth with a combination of certain chemicals, heat and pressure. Clues to identification are contained in the size, color and shape of the inclusions inside the stone.

SYNTHETIC STONES are made by man in a laboratory using the same combination of chemicals, heat and pressure. They are the same physically, chemically and optically as the natural. Laboratory grown crystals also yield clues as to their origin. During the 1920 & 30's synthetic stones were used to compliment some of the finest natural gemstones. With a few exceptions such as the CZ, synthetic stones have a natural counter-part.

IMITATION STONES can be any material that is used to imitate a stone. This can be anything ranging from glass to plastic. Imitations can be made any color of the rainbow.

Just because a piece is old do not fall into the trap of believing that it must be real. Imitation stones date back to the Egyptians. After 30 years of dealing with antique jewelry I am still amazed at what I find. Let's look at some of these stones.

DIAMONDS

Diamonds have been known throughout history as the invincible stone. Early warriors wore them into battle in the belief that it would protect them. Today the diamond is known as the traditional stone to signify an intent of marriage and as a seal for the wedding vows.

The value of a diamond is determined by factors known as the "4 C's" - carat, clarity, color & cut. Let's take a brief look at each of these.

Carat: The weight of a stone is measured in metric carats. There are 100 points in a carat. But do not look for 100 tiny points in a diamond any more than you would look for 100 pennies in a dollar bill. Each point is one hundredth of a metric carat. Consequently 50 points would be one-half carat and 25 points would be one-fourth of a carat.

Remember that "carat" is a weight not a size. Two diamonds each weighing a carat can be very different in size according to the way they are cut. One may be smaller in diameter but its top and bottom portions may be higher and deeper. If a one carat diamond is cut to "Ideal" proportions the girdle (see diagram) will be approximately 6.5mm in diameter.

V-1; Having stressed the fact that you cannot always tell the weight of a diamond by its diameter, I still use this clear plastic weight estimator template for a rough gauge of size.

If all other factors (the other 3 C's) are equal the bigger the diamond the more valuable. Consequently a one carat diamond is much more valuable than ten, 10 point diamonds.

Clarity: The clarity of a diamond is measured by the amount of or lack of inclusions or flaws on the outside or inside of the stone. Because I am a Graduate Gemologist, I use the grading system used by the Gemological Institute of America. It is accepted as a standard throughout the world.

> ***Flawless*** - This designation is only given to stones without any flaws or inclusions on the outside or inside of the stone. They are rare.
>
> ***IF*** - Internally Flawless means that there are not any internal inclusions, but there is something on the outside of the stone.
>
> ***VV S1*** - very, very slightly included.
>
> ***VV S2*** - one step down in clarity.
>
> ***V S1*** - Very slightly included.
>
> ***V S2*** - one step down in clarity.
>
> ***S I1*** - slightly included.
>
> ***S I2*** - one step down in clarity.
>
> ***I1*** - Inclusions, chips, cavities, etc., visible to the un-aided eye.

Diamond clarity grading should be done with a 10X loupe under dark field illumination.

Color: Color or the absence of it is the next "C". The GIA color grading system for diamonds begins with the letter "D" and continues through the alphabet to the letter "Z". Letters at the beginning of this scale are colorless or near colorless. As the letters progress so does the amount of color. Most people associate color with degrees of yellow but a diamond can also be "off-color" to the brown or gray tone.

Because most people prefer stones that "face-up" white, the demand for "off-color" stones is minimal. However, when the depth of color becomes intense and vivid toward the end of the scale, the colored diamond becomes more valuable than the colorless. Natural fancy colored diamonds are some of the rarest gems in the world. Believe it or not they are found in all the colors of the rainbow. Most people are surprised to read that they can be so colorful, but almost everyone knows that the Hope Diamond in the Smithsonian Institution is blue and that the "Tiffany" is yellow.

Today "off-color" diamonds can be bombarded or irridated to change the color to blue, green, yellow or brown. Obviously, these are valued at a small percentage of their natural counterparts.

The color grade of a stone is always determined by looking through the pavilion of the stone. Consequently, mounted stones are much more difficult to color grade.

Cut: The last "C" is the one that most people know the least about. It is most important because a diamond cut to ideal proportions will appear to be a better color and clarity grade.

Brilliance is the return of the white light to the eye. Everyone wants a "brilliant" white diamond. The brilliance is returned through the table. A poorly cut stone can "leak" light from other areas and diminish the brilliance.

If you've ever seen a diamond that seems to shoot out colors of gold, green, blue and orange-red, you have seen what is known as "dispersion". This is the breaking up of the white light into its "spectral colors". In my opinion a well cut stone "sings & dances".

Dispersion is determined by the crown angles. If the stone is spread cut to make it appear larger the crown angles suffer and dispersion is lost.

Cut can also refer to the shape of a stone. Whether the stone is a marquis, pear, princess, emerald or round cut is a factor in determining value. Some shapes are more expensive than others.

The primary consideration for a purchase should be which shape is most complimentary to the area on which it will be worn and the preferences of the individual wearing it.

Gemologists/appraisers judge all four factors to determine value. To better understand what is known as a round brilliant cut, the following diagram is provided.

It is important to know the basic parts of a diamond, because the "table", "cutlet" and "girdle" size can all provide clues to when a stone might have been cut and if it could be original to the mounting.

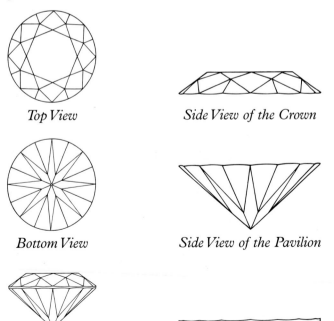

Top View   *Side View of the Crown*

Bottom View   *Side View of the Pavilion*

Side view of the Stone   *Girdle*

TESTING DIAMONDS

If you have a loose clear stone and want to know whether or not it is a diamond there are some simple tests that may help in this determination.

For the first test draw a line on a sheet of white paper. Place the stone (table down) on the line. If the stone is a diamond, the line will not be visible. Any other clear stone will allow the line to show through. (See photo **#V-1**).

The next test is done by placing the stone on a sheet of white paper and holding a penlight under it. Be sure that the light shines up under the stone. If the stone is a CZ, YAG, or any other clear stone, the light will outline the stone and also show through the middle. If the stone is a diamond, the outline will show through but the middle will remain dark.

Another test is the "breath test". If breathing on the stone causes it to "fog" this is an indication that the stone in question is <u>not</u> a diamond.

These tests should be performed for the first time using stones that are known. This provides a chance to see the accurate reactions before testing an unknown stone.

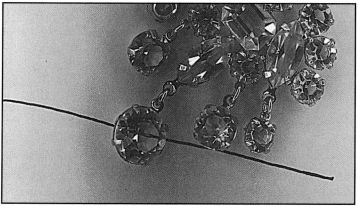

V-1; This necklace has open-backed round brilliant cut stones. By placing it on a line drawn on a piece of paper you can see immediately that the stones are not diamonds. This photo shows the stone "table up". The test should be done "table down". The line shows through just as clearly but it is broken up into several straight lines. If this stone was a diamond, the line would not be visible through the pavilion in a table down position.

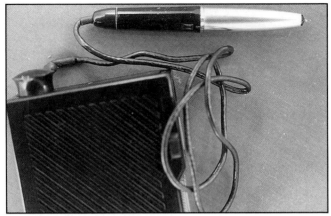

V-1; *My diamond tester. What you can't see is the gauge that goes from simulant to diamond.*

Diamonds are the most heat conductive stone. An amazingly accurate determination of whether or not a stone is a diamond can be done with a portable tool that takes advantage of this fact. This battery operated diamond tester has a probe that heats up. If the point makes contact with a diamond the stone conducts the heat away from the point and it registers "diamond". A diamond tester of this type is usually priced at about $140.00.

MOISSANITE

This is a new stone that looks like a diamond. Anyone in the business should be on the look out for these stones. Some are even set in antique mountings to scam people. To make matters even worse, Moissanite is heat conductive and a diamond tester will register it as a diamond. Although Moissanite is a natural stone, it is synthetically produced in volume for commercial use.

TESTS FOR MOISSANITE

If a stone looks suspicious after being tested by a probe, I always use an instrument that will test the electrical and electronic properties of the stone. Moissanite is heat & electrically conductive. Moissanite detectors are more expensive than a diamond tester but they do come in handy to insure a stone that tests as a diamond is truly a diamond. A combination moissanite and diamond detector will soon be available for under $180.00. Stay tuned!

Women's Modern Rings~ Brilliant White Synthetic Sapphires or Red Synthetic Rubies

All Set in High Quality Mountings

SYNTHETIC stones are real gems artificially formed in laboratories instead of by nature. Made of the same elements and in much the same way—chemically compounded by extreme heat—the synthetic by electric furnaces, the genuine by nature before the earth cooled. Their color, brilliancy and hardness is identical but you find less imperfections in the synthetic stones.

To Find Correct Ring Size, See Page 345

Your Choice
Solid 18 Karat White Gold

$9.98

BEAUTIFUL mountings in dainty pierced design of 18-Karat white gold—same patterns and quality used for diamonds. The sparkling synthetic sapphires and rubies are alive with color rivaling natural stones for brilliancy. Our prices are exceedingly low for such marvelous quality. Each ring in handsome presentation case. State size. Postpaid.

(A) SOLID 18-Karat white gold with ¼-Carat size stone full of brilliancy and sparkle.

545 C 5900—
Synthetic white sapphire.
545 C 5901—
Synthetic red ruby.
Each............$9.98

(B) Pierced design mounting of 18-Karat solid white gold with ¼-Carat size synthetic sapphire or ruby. State size.

545 C 5908—
Synthetic white sapphire.
545 C 5913—
Synthetic red ruby.
Each............$9.98

(C) Two almond shaped white synthetic sapphires one on each side of ¼-Carat synthetic stone in 18-K solid white gold setting.

545 C 5934—
Synthetic white sapphire.
545 C 5935—
Synthetic red ruby.
Each............$9.98

Attractive Gift Cases

Your Choice
Beautiful Synthetic Sapphires

$12.98

18-K. solid white gold, in pierced design. ¼-Carat white synthetic sapphire in center with two blue triangular synthetic sapphires on sides. State ring size. Postpaid.

18-K. solid white gold; 1-Ct. stone in center, two small synthetic rubies on sides. State ring size. Postpaid.

545 C 6173 —Synthetic white sapphire............$12.98
545 C 6196 —Synthetic red ruby. Postpaid $12.98
545 C 5904 ....$12.98

Three Popular Rings
Brilliant Synthetic White Sapphires

BEAUTIFUL synthetic white sapphires set in high class rings, especially designed to reflect the modern styles in ring creation. Solid white gold—exactly the same quality and artistically pierced designs that are used with diamonds. Handsome gift case included. Be sure to state finger size. We Pay Postage.

(A) Synthetic white sapphire, ¼-Carat size. Solid 18-Karat white gold mounting in attractive pierced design.
545 C 5905—
............$7.98

(B) Synthetic white sapphire, ¼-Carat size, in dainty solid white gold ring.
545 C 6168—
14-Karat......$5.25
545 C 6167—
18-Karat......$6.25

(C) Brilliant ¼-Carat Synthetic white sapphire set in dainty solid white gold mounting.
545 C 6163—
14-Karat......$3.85
545 C 6164—
18-Karat......$4.50

To Find Correct Ring Size, See Page 345

V-A; An advertisement from the 1931-32 Montgomery Wards catalogue.

Because Moissanite is <u>doubly</u> refractive, a person experienced with a loupe can detect "doubling through the pavillion facets". Diamonds are <u>singularly</u> refractive.

TESTING SYNTHETIC DIAMONDS

Industrial quality synthetic diamonds were perfected in 1955. Gem quality synthetic diamonds have been possible since 1970. Synthetic diamonds are grown in a laboratory using the same heat and pressure as those buried beneath the ground. They have almost all the qualities of a natural diamond. Consequently a diamond tester will also register positive for this stone. If the synthetic diamond is grown by the nickel catalyst method they have an electronic property that can be detected by some Moissanite detectors.

TESTING SAPPHIRES & RUBIES

Sapphires and rubies are both "corundum". It comes in every color of the rainbow and all the colors except red are known as sapphires. The red ones are know as rubies. Because sapphires are heat conductors, both natural and synthetic sapphires and rubies will make the needle move on a diamond tester such as the one shown in photo *#V-I*. It will not go over to the "diamond" side of the gauge but it will move. During the 1920's & 30's, synthetic white sapphires were used in engagement rings and wedding sets. The Wards Catalog for fall and winter 1931-1932 featured synthetic white sapphire sets in 18k white gold filigree. (see page #73)

Inclusions or the lack thereof can help separate synthetic from natural corundum. The first synthetic ruby came on to the market in the late 1800's. When I tell some people that their great-grandmother's ring is set with a synthetic ruby, they do not want to believe it. This early method of synthesizing rubies produced good colored stones without any inclusions. This lack of inclusion should be a good clue that the stone is man made. A good size natural ruby without any inclusion is very rare.

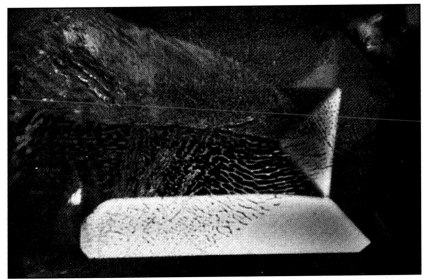

V-2; Synthetic ruby magnified to show flux inclusion.

A few years ago I went to Bangkok as a jewelry consultant. The people who hired me were tired of going to Asia and coming back with man-made sapphires and rubies. One gentleman was in the market for a star ruby or star sapphire ring. We took a tour of a gem-cutting factory which conveniently ended in their jewelry showroom. Every star ruby and star sapphire man's ring we looked at was synthetic. I asked the sales lady if all these stones were synthetic. "All we have are natural stones", she replied. Their synthetic stones were easily detected by their curved growth lines on the bottom of the cabochon cut stone. Natural sapphires and rubies have straight lines or hexagonal growth.

TESTING ZIRCONS

Zircon in its natural and synthetic form has often been used as a substitute for diamonds. It was very popular around the turn of the century and throughout the 1920's & 30's.

Colorless zircons can be mistaken for diamonds. Because they are highly doubly refractive they are fairly easy to detect with a 10X loupe and a little practice.

First look through the stone and focus on a facet in the pavilion area. Note the line where 2 facets join together. Slowly tilt the stone back and forth. If it is a doubly refractive stone the lines will split apart and come back together or double. I suggest going to a Gem & Mineral Show and purchasing a small synthetic zircon for practice purposes. Look under "Test for Other Stones" in this Chapter for other doubly refractive stones.

PASTE "STONES"

George Ravenscroft developed flint glass which was referred to as lead glass in 1675. But the name most associated with paste is Frederick Strauss, who developed a formula of leaded glass that soon became so popular that Louis XV gave his mistress a set of blue paste earrings. The Strauss factory was in production from 1730 to 1773. Strauss' death did not stop the use of paste. Many beautiful pieces were made. The original paste pieces were done in silver and unlike the stones of this day most of them were in closed or a combination of closed and open backs. In 18th Century pieces the stones should be old mine cut.

Genuine paste is still made today in Austria, France and Czechoslovakia. Old paste is quite expensive and is getting hard to find. In the summer of 1999, I purchased a pair of paste earrings, circa 1830's-40's set in silver. I was happy to get them for $400.00. Collectors love paste jewelry for its beauty and the history it holds. Because diamond jewelry was often re-mounted as fashions changed, paste pieces are often beautiful examples of the jewelry of its time period.

Many people refer to any stone in costume jewelry as paste. This is not true.

RHINESTONES

These are another imitator of diamonds. Again, the term is loosely used for any glass stones in costume jewelry, so much so that it has been commonly accepted. The name rhinestones originally meant the colorless rock crystal stones that were found in the River Rhine. If they were purple they would be amethyst and if golden they would be citrine. They are all quartz. The colorless crystals were cut in the brilliant style to imitate diamonds.

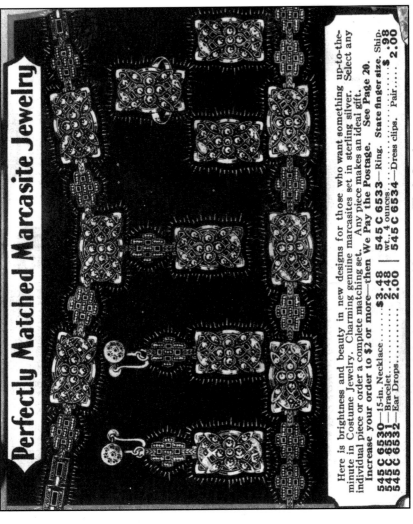

Perfectly Matched Marcasite Jewelry

Here is brightness and beauty in new designs for those who want something up-to-the-minute in Costume Jewelry. Charming genuine marcasites set in sterling silver. Select any individual piece or order a complete matching set. Any piece makes an ideal gift. Increase your order to $2 or more—then We Pay the Postage.   See Page 20.

545 C 6530—15-in. Necklace......$3.48 | 545 C 6533—Ring. State finger size. Ship.
545 C 6531—Bracelet.............. 2.48 | wt., 4 ounces.................. $ .98
545 C 6532—Ear Drops........... 2.00 | 545 C 6534—Dress clips. Pair..... 2.00

V-3; Marcasite Jewelry for sale in the 1931-32 Montgomery Wards Catalogue.

MARCASITE

Marcasites were fashionable substitutes for diamonds as early as the 1700's. They were always mounted in silver as were the diamonds of the period. In the mid 1800's they once again were in favor. The fashion waned until the glittering mood of the twenties revived it again.

The "stone" known as marcasite is actually pyrite (PIE-rite). There is a mineral named marcasite, and, although it is similar in appearance, it is not suitable for jewelry. This case of mistaken identity is now commonly accepted. The iron sulfite, pyrite is cut into small pointed or rounded facets to create marcasites. Since their luster is metallic, their brilliance comes from light reflecting off the facets.

Better marcasite jewelry has stones that are actually set with prongs or beads. In less expensive pieces they are glued in. It often takes an examination with a loupe to make this determination because although some pieces often have the small "beads" of metal used to hold the stone, a closer look will reveal that the beads are not even touching the marcasite. The metal the "stones" are in and the design of the piece are also factors that greatly influence prices.

Marcasites are also immitated in plastic, but the Jewelry Detective "teeth test" will help detect them. These imitations can date back to the 1920's. There are many new marcasite pieces on the market. Buying from a reputable dealer who will guarantee in writing the age of the piece, is the best assurance for the new collector.

TESTING GLASS

Moldavite and obsidian are both natural glass but they are not usually used as a substitute for other stones.

Man-made glass is a mixture of sand, potash or soda and lead or lime. These ingredients are artificially fused together and then cooled before they can crystallize. Glass can be made in any color and can be transparent or opaque. It has been used for centuries to imitate all types of stones.

V-3; Brooch c.1840's set with glass "amethyst".

V-4; Orange peel effect on glass.

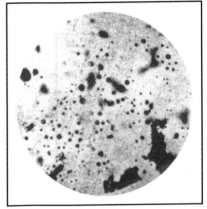

V-5; Round gas bubbles.

V-6; Gas bubbles.

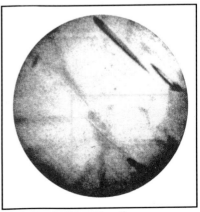

V-7; Gas bubble with tail.

It is surprising where and in what mountings glass "stones" are placed. Photo **#V-3** shows the front of a well made brooch circa 1840's. It is rolled gold and the amethyst colored "stone" is glass. Amethyst are relatively inexpensive stones ranging in price today from about $7.00 to $20.00 per carat. One would naturally assume that the "stone" was genuine. Not true!

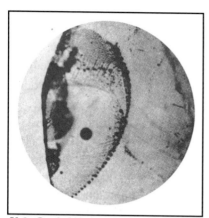

V-8; Gas bubble in a feather-like formation.

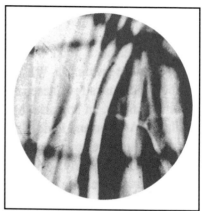

V-9; Swirl marks and flow lines sometimes seen in glass used to imitate gemstones.

Many 10k yellow gold rings from the 1940's were set with glass "stones". Be on the look-out for clues to their identity. Photo **#V-4** is magnified to show the "orange peel" effect and concave facets indicative of glass. Other clues are bubbles found in man-made materials. They can be round or shaped as if the circle had been pulled sometimes even including a "tail". (See figure **#V-5-#V-7**). They can also occur close together in a feather-like formation as shown in photo **#V-8.**

Curved swirls or curved lines are also clues that the material in question is glass. (Figure **#V-9**)

ALEXANDRITE

This chapter would be incomplete if I didn't mention synthetic alexandrite-like corundum. Almost every week I get a telephone call from someone who tells me that they have an alexandrite. I immediately ask them how large it is and they usually tell me that it is large. Next I ask what colors does it display and the reply is always "blue and purple". Armed with these clues I can determine that the stone is not alexandrite.

If it were a large alexandrite it would be very valuable. I've never seen a huge one. More importantly a true alexandrite changes color from red to green according to the type of light under which it is viewed.

Synthetic alexandrite-like corundum has been used for years. It is found in Mexican silver jewelry and 10k and 14k gold pieces. Now you know the "rest of the story".

DOUBLETS AND TRIPLETS

Before relatively inexpensive synthetic stones were available, a combination stone called a "doublet" was popular. The lapidary fused a layer of one stone to another, then faceted the stone as if it were one large stone. The most popular doublet was one using garnet and glass. It was used to imitate sapphires, topaz, emeralds, amethyst, rubies and garnets in the 19th and early 20th centuries.

The garnet top is harder than glass and it makes the stone more resistant to scratches. A piece of green or blue glass with a red garnet top is intriguing. It takes a trained eye and close inspection to detect. Consequently, pieces of jewelry set with old doublets are quite collectable. Most people are fascinated by them.

Garnet and glass doublets can be identified by looking through the top of the stone with a 10X loupe. A clue is an irregular circular line that is not a part of the facets or table. This is the garnet cap. Under this area and around the "table" look for numerous gas bubbles all on the same plane (level) of depth in the stone. These were formed as the garnet cap was fused to the glass bottom.

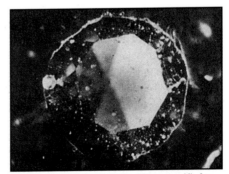

V-10: *Garnet & glass doublet magnified to show the garnet cap and gas bubbles.*

The term "triplet" is used to describe a stone that is made up of three parts. This can mean three stones (genuine top and bottom with something else in between), or it can refer to two stones put together with a colored cement that provides the "stone's" color. Because synthetic emeralds are expensive, triplets made of quartz or synthetic spinel joined by emerald green cement are often encountered.

A simple test for these "joined" stones is to immerse the suspect in water. Because of the different light refraction in the water you should be able to distinguish the joints.

OTHER TESTS FOR STONES

The first test for any stone is visual. Get your 10 power loupe and look at the stone. There are many things to notice. When examining colored stones, look for color zoning. In layman's terms this is a variance of color, usually there is more color or more intense color in some areas of the stone. This "zoning" (especially noticeable in amethyst) is an indication of a natural stone. Synthetic stones usually have more "life" and are evenly colored.

When examining the cut of a stone, notice whether or not the facets have sharp, precise lines. Natural stones have to be cut to their best advantage and are not always as precise as synthetic ones. Look for signs of layers that could mean a doublet or triplet. Chips and Abrasions on the surface of a clear stone are usually an indication that the stone is not a diamond.

Next look <u>into</u> the stone. Natural stones often have needle-like angular inclusions. Synthetics have curved lines or curved color bandings. Any stone made by a flame fusion process such as glass and some synthetics will usually have round gas or air bubbles.

Another more difficult test is one for "refraction". This is done by looking through the stone and focusing on a pavilion facet line (where two facets intersect). Slowly tilt the stone back and forth. If one looks like two or splits apart and comes back together, it is a doubly refractive stone. Peridot, topaz, tourmaline, emerald, quartz, amethyst, citrine, synthetic rutile and zircon are all double refractive stones. The last two are highly refractive and can often be identified by this test alone. Diamonds, garnets, spinels and glass do not double refract. Although this test does not give all the answers, its results are well worth the effort to become proficient.

There are many other tests used by the gemologist to determine stones. Synthetics have become so sophisticated that even an expert cannot be sure without the aid of expensive equipment. Today a trained gemologist with a well-equipped laboratory is imperative for proper stone identification.

This is not to say that the average person cannot learn to identify and enjoy stones. The best way to gain this knowledge is by becoming visually acquainted with the various stones. Take every opportunity to view and examine them. Antique Shows and Gem and Mineral Shows provide ideal opportunities to handle stones. Most dealers and participants are more than willing to share their knowledge.

Some stones such a malachite, lapis, turquoise, bloodstone and carnelian can be visually identified. Gemstones of the World by Walter Schumann is filled with true-color photos that help with visual identifications. (see order form in the back of this book)

The clues contained in this chapter will help you decide if professional help is needed. Many gemologists will charge as little as $15.00 for a stone test. If the stone then warrants an appraisal this charge is usually deducted from the appraisal charge.

It will pay you in the long run to get acquainted with a graduate gemologist-appraiser. Don't be afraid to ask questions such as "Are you a Graduate Gemologist? Have you had special training for appraising new and antique jewelry? How do you determine the charge for your appraisal?"

Call at least three appraisers before deciding on the one to use. If you are a dealer, collector or just own a lot of jewelry it is important to have an appraiser that communicates well; one that makes you feel comfortable. Trust and communication is always important but even more so in a situation in which you may be leaving your jewelry.

THE EVOLUTION OF DIAMOND CUTS

Diamonds have mystified and fascinated people throughout the ages. But it has literally taken centuries for the cut of the stone to be perfected to display the sparkle and brilliance of which they are capable. The following is a short version of the evolution of the diamond cuts. It is by no means complete but hopefully it will help you recognize and identify the different cuts that may be encountered. Remember these cuts were also used for other gemstones and even imitation "stones".

Ancient - Point Cut
In ancient times the sides of the natural uncut octahedral were polished and the stone was mounted in that form. This is known as the "point cut".

V-11; Natural uncut diamond octahedral.

14th - 15th Century Table Cut
Somewhere in the years between 1330 and 1475 the table cut was introduced. The natural points of the octahedral crystal were removed forming a table at the top and a cutlet at the bottom.

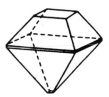

Top View 　　　　*Bottom View* 　　　　*Side View*

16th Century Sancy Cut

A famous diamond called the "Grand Sancy" was cut in this style (c.1593). It was pear shaped with rose cut style facets and a 5 sided table. It has a fascinating history. Well worth the time to look it up in the Illustrated Dictionary of Jewelry.

17th Century Rose Cut

Around 1620 the rose cut became popular. A flat bottomed "Macle" diamond is used for this cut. The top is faceted with triangles that come to a point at the center of the stone. Cutters loved this style because they could do so many variations in the number of facets. They were cut in circles, ovals and elliptical shapes.

Top View

Side View

Rose Cut

Top View

Side View

V-12; Rose cut garnet in a 1880's necklace.

Mazarin Cut - Mid 1600's

Named after Cardinal Mazarin, this diamond cut (c.1650) features 34 facets. It was a rather "blocky" looking forerunner of today's "brilliant cut".

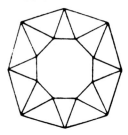

Top View   *Side View*

18th Century

Peruzzi Cut

This cut is said to have been named for the Venetian lapidary who invented it around 1700. This "cushion" cut had a table, a cutlet and 56 facets on the crown and pavilion making it the original "Brilliant Cut".

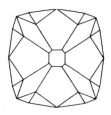

Top View   *Side View*   *Bottom View*

18th & 19th Century Old Mine Cut

As you can see the mine cut is the same as the Peruzzi. Many people have the misconception that it was called the mine cut because it was literally cut at the mine. Not true! Diamonds cut in this style were from the Brazilian mines discovered in the early 1700. When new mines were discovered in South Africa (c.1867), the mines in Brazil became known as the "old mines". After the invention of the bruting machine (1891) diamonds could have a round girdle. It was associated with the new African stones. Stones with the squarish girdle outline were referred to as the "old mine cut".

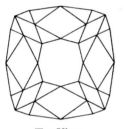 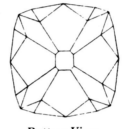 

Top View   *Bottom View*   *Side View*

19th Century & Early 20th Century

Old European Cut

After the bruting machine was invented (1891) the girdle of the old mine cut was rounded to make what is referred to as an Old European Cut.

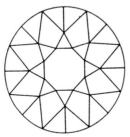 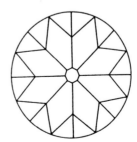

Top View   *Bottom View*

V-13; Rock crystal stone showing the small table and high crown angle associated with Old European Cut Stone (c.1890's set in sterling silver).

Briolette Cut

This old cut became popular again in the late 19th and early 20th century. As you can see it was the perfect cut for earrings and pendants. An elongated version of the rose cut, it was used for all types of stones from diamonds to glass during these years. The oldest diamond in recorded history was the Briolette of India (c.1150).

Version 1-Side View

Version 2-Side View

20th Century-Modern Brilliant Cut

The brilliant cut has 32 facets above the "girdle" plus the table, 24 below the girdle, and sometimes a cutlet. (See diagram under "Diamonds"). If cut to ideal proportions the white light will be returned to the eye, thus insuring the brilliant cut stone to look "brilliant".

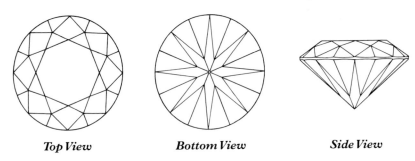

Top View   *Bottom View*   *Side View*

Buff Cut

This cut features a smooth cabochon top and a facet pavilion. It was popular in the late 19th and the first half of the 20th century. A version of this cut is also popular for class rings.

Side View

19th & 20th Century Single Cut

This cut is usually used on very small diamonds under .05 carats. An older version of this cut has a squarish girdle outline and is known as the 8 cut.

   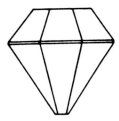   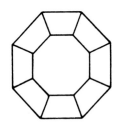

Top View   *Side View*   *Eight Cut Top*

V-14; Compare the cut of the center stone to the single cut diagram on the preceding page.

This necklace has open backed stones and are not foiled but a good Jewelry Detective would know at a glance that the stones are not diamonds. How? The "stones" are single cut and diamonds this large would never be cut this way.

Baguette
This cut usually used for smaller side stones was especially popular in the 1920's-30's time period. It lent itself well to the Art Deco style of straight machine cut lines.

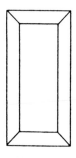
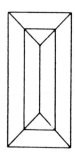

Top View   *Bottom View*

This type baguette was another version of this cut. Both types are still popular today.

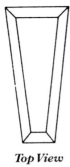 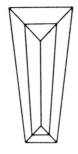

Top View   *Bottom View*

Emerald Cut
Although this cut was developed in the late 1800's, it took the demand of the geometric shapes of the Art Deco style to bring it to prominence. Note how the sides are "step cut."

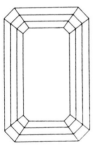 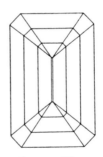 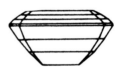

Top View   *Bottom View*   *Side View*

Scissors Cut
This is a version of the Emerald or Step Cut. It is also known as the Cross-Cut. This cut can be square or rectangular.

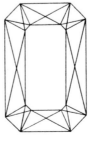 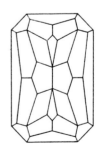

Top View   *Bottom View*

Modern Variations of the Brilliant Cut.

Pear Shape-Top View

Pear Shape-Bottom View

Heart Shape-Top View

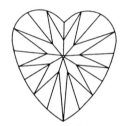

Heart Shape-Bottom View

Marquis Cut

This boat shaped modified brilliant cut is also known as a "Navette" cut.

Marquis Cut-Top View

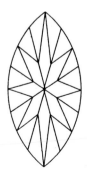

Marquis Cut-Bottom View

This shape became popular after 1955 when Lazare Kaplan & Sons of New York trademarked and advertised the name "Oval Elegance".

 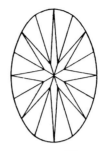

Top View   *Bottom View*

Princess Cut
This cut was developed in 1961.

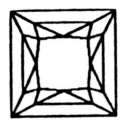

Top View

Chapter VI

Fittings & Findings
Circa Dating Clues

The back of a piece of jewelry can often provide as many or more clues than the front. The fittings and findings can help circa date the piece, tell something about its quality and reveal additions or alterations.

Findings are ready made pieces that jewelers use such as clasps, pin stems, hinges, ear ring studs, etc.

VI-1A; Back view with the pin stem removed and the C clasp removed.

VI-1B; View of the pin stem assembly attached. Note how the pendant loop swirls to the side.

Fittings refer to these parts and more that are custom made for a piece. They can range from something as simple as a necklace hook attachment to something as complicated as pin stems and hinges that screw off; or "c" clasp that folds down to convert a brooch into a pendant. (see *#VI-1A, B & C*) These custom made "fittings" are a clue that it was extremely well made and usually an expensive piece of jewelry.

This chapter includes some basic fittings and findings that can help you circa date pieces.

VI-1C; Victorian stone cameo brooch/pendant. Frank Axelrod Antiques.

First let's look at the clasps. The "C" clasp is the earliest type of catch, but it can sometimes be found on new jewelry.

 This early safety was used on pins dating from the 1890's - 1910.

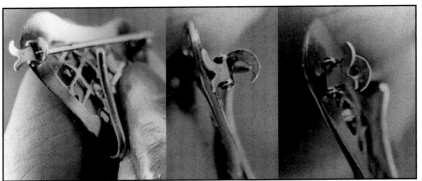

VI-2; Watch pin with the early safety catch.

Before safety clasps were developed another back-up pin was used for safety. Photos *#VI-3* & *VI-4* shows a brooch c.1840 - 50's - with a chain and pin attached by a small ring. When you encounter a brooch with the small ring you can be assured that the brooch originally had a safety attachment such as this.

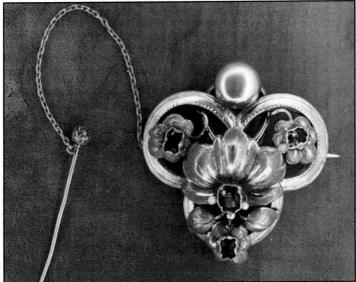

VI-3; An attached stick pin adds a safety feature to this brooch.

VI-4; *Back view. Note the small ring at the top from which the chain and stick pin are suspended.*

For a later example (c.1890's - 1900) see photos **#VI-5** & **VI-6**.

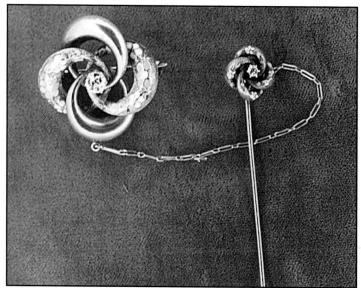

VI-5; *As the century drew closer to it's end, the safety attachment became a part of the overall design of the brooch.*

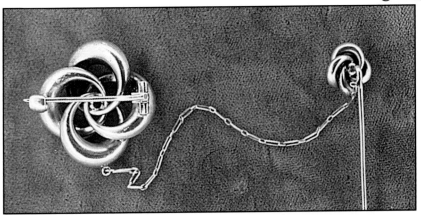

VI-6; *Back view.*

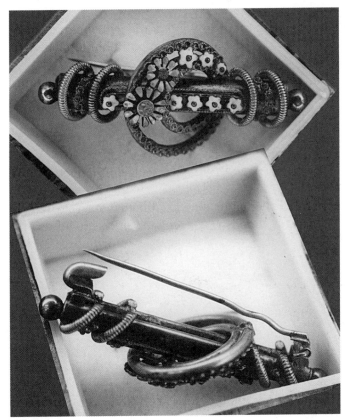

VI-7

The new popular safety pin head was also put to use as a safety.

Although the safety pin was patented in the mid 1800's, it wasn't used in jewelry until the 1880 - 1890's. The enameled brooch has the safety pin "head" indicating its time period. (See Photo **#VI-7**)

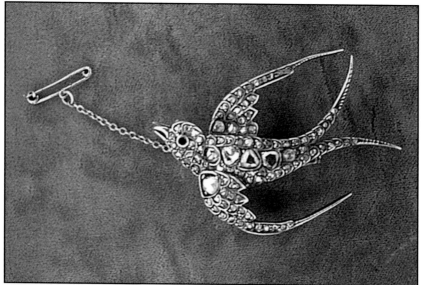

VI-8; Diamond Brooch c.1880 with safety pin attachment.

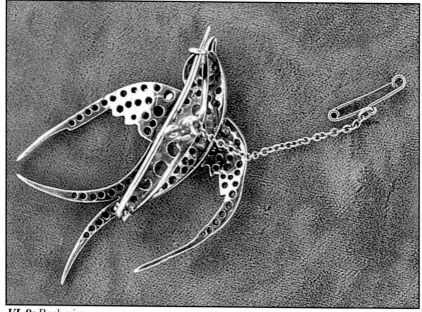

VI-9; Back view.

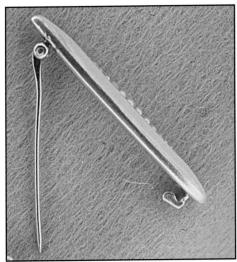

VI-10; Enamel pin c.1890's with a safety pin catch.

Open

I have found this type of catch on European pieces as early as 1896, but my research indicates they were not generally used in the United States before 1912. They continued to be popular through the 1920's. (See *#VII-11*)

VI-11; Safety catch on filigree brooch c.1920's.

The tube or trombone type clasp was used at the end of the 19th century and continued to be used in Europe through the 1940's. (see photo *#VI-12 on opposite page*)

VI-12; Trombone catch.

This type safety clasp became popular in the 1920's and is still used today. Often the new safety clasp was added to old pieces. This allowed people to wear their old family pieces without fear of loss.

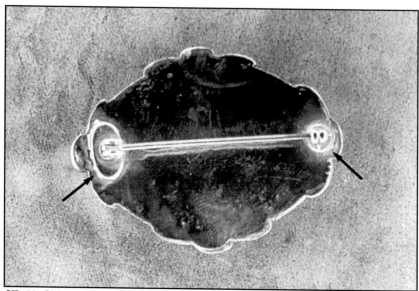

VI-13; Safety with oval attachment pad. This pad is a sure sign of a replacement catch.

Sometimes new hinges were also added. The brooch in photo **#VI-13** (c1840's) has had the pin stem shortened and a new hinge and clasp added. The clue to the addition are the small metal pads behind the findings. These made it easy to solder the piece on and it was particularly suited to "soft soldering". This soft solder is used on pieces that can not withstand heat. For instance a piece containing pearls or a cameo or any material or stone that will not withstand the higher temperature that it takes for a "hard-solder".

Hinges

Hinges are less complicated. There are only 2 types that you will probably encounter.

 The tube hinge which was used until approximately 1890's is just what the name implies. The pin stem is attached to the center tube and is set between the 2 end tubes which are stationary.

A pin goes through all 3 tubes and holds the pin stem in place while allowing it to fold back for attachment.

 In the 1890's a newer hinge was developed. This smaller trimmer version that could easily be reproduced became immediately popular. It is still used today.

 This one piece pin stem assembly is often used on inexpensive pieces. It is also popular with "hobbiest" because it can be glued on to a variety of materials. It would be quite unusual to find this type on a valuable piece of jewelry.

Ear Ring Findings

The shepherd crook or fish hook is an early type of ear wire. It is also used today.

 Kidney wires have been used since the 1870's. They are still popular today.

 New Version of the kidney wire.

  These 2 types of lever backs are still in vogue today.

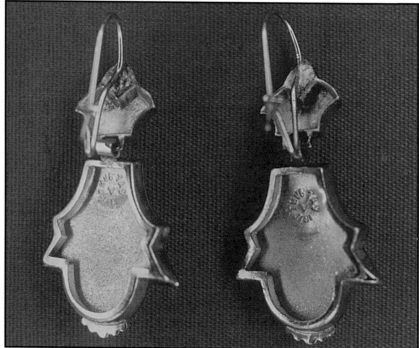

VI-14; (Circa 1870 earrings with replacement kidney wires. Note the soft solder "blobs" at the top. Even though the earrings are gold, soft solder was used because they are set with stone cameos and embellished with black Taille' d Epergne enamel which would have been damaged by the heat from a "hard" solder.

The threaded studs are circa 1890's. They are used today, but are smaller in diameter and the nut is usually a lighter weight than the older versions.

Eventually studs evolved to a thinner diameter and a friction nut replaced the threaded screws.

Screw Back unpierced earrings became popular in 1909. They are still made today but they are not common on new pieces.

Screw type earrings did not offer the security of the pierced earrings. Consequently an industrious soul invented what was known as the "earring guard". The patent # is 1,582,383. Look the number up on page #60 and you'll solve the mystery of when it was introduced.

Clips date from 1940 - 1950 and are still used on some new earrings.

Bracelet Catches

This box clasp is an early form that is still used today.

Back View

This style foldover catch is usually associated with less expensive jewelry.

The foldover style with a built in safety was very popular for watches. They can be found on expensive and inexpensive pieces.

This built in safety feature was used in the 1890's in bangle bracelets. The small end is attached inside one side of the bracelet tube and the hook fit into the other. This allows the hinged bangle to open wide enough to go over the hand and on to the arm but still keeps it from falling off if the clasp accidentally opens.

Probably the most interesting period for bracelet and watch clasps was the 1920's - 1930's. In these years inventors went wild trying to out do each other with built-in safetys. It's sometimes hard for today's generation to figure out how to open them. Many of them are so ingenious that I wonder why they are not used today.

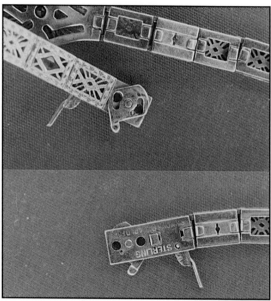

VI-15; This bracelet c.1930's has a very complicated safety clasp.

Today the lobster style clasp, the spring ring and toggle clasp are popular for costume and fine jewelry.

Lobster clasp   *Spring ring*   *Toggle clasp*

Swivel Findings

VI-16; Swivel closed   *VI-17; Swivel open*

A swivel is used at the end of a watch chain to attach the pocket watch. This early (c.1840's) style unscrews and folds out to go through the "bow" of the watch.

This style swivel was popular in the late 19th century and continues to be used today. A top portion of the oval loop can be pushed open to go over the "bow" of the watch and then it springs back into place.

VI-18   *VI-19; T-bar*

Photo *#VI-18* shows an example of an inexpensive version of a watch clasp. It does not swivel and does not offer nearly as much security for the watch.

Pendant Loops

In the early 20th century this fitting became popular. It attaches to a brooch and makes it into a brooch/pendant combination. The top illustration is the type pendant swivel loop that is used by the manufacturer when it is original. The bottom one was used as an addition to a finished piece. Note the soldering pad.

Front view   *Side view*

This style locket or pendant loop is just pushed in at the back (see side view) to enable it to go over the pendant or locket ring. They are available in many variations of this theme.

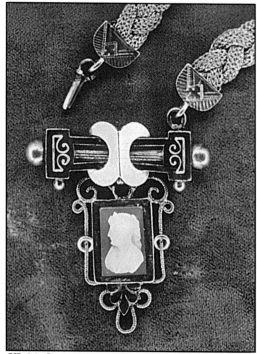

Misc. Findings

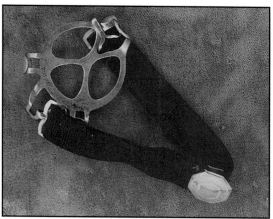

VI-20

This funny looking bracelet was used to convert a small pendant watch into a wrist watch.

This Victorian necklace is a good example of how the necklaces of the period were secured. Obviously, the designers knew back in the 1860 - 80's that women didn't have eyes in the back of their head.

VI-21; *Stone cameo necklace. Note the tongue of the clasp fits into the top of the pendant.*

VI-22; Stone cameo brooch.

VI-23; Side view showing opening for original pendant attachment.

Knowing this fact, makes it easier to solve the mystery of why the brooch has a "catch" hole at the top. (See photos *#VI-22* & *VI-23*) This is a pendant drop that was converted to be used as a brooch.

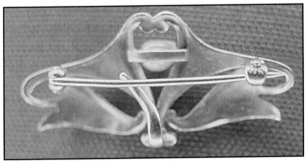

VI-24

This pin with a "hook" in the middle of the back is known as a watch pin. The hook often has enough "crook" in it to help secure the pendant watch.

Even though we looked at Duette brooches in Chapter II a chapter on fittings and findings would not be complete without their inclusion.

VI-25; Front view of brooch.

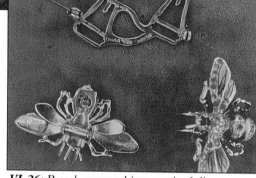

VI-26; Brooch converted into a pair of clips.

In the mid 1800's "revolving" brooches became popular. The piece in photo *#VI-27A* shows a tin type of a man turned to the back. A palette worked curl of hair is on the other side. The owner could wear it either way. It was like having 2 brooches for the price of 1.

VI-27A; Back view of a revolving brooch.   *VI-27B; Tin type turned to the front.*
Note that the original pin stem extends
beyond the body of the pin. This is indicative
of the time period.

Fittings

It is interesting to see the imagination that went into fittings on older pieces. This pendant (c.1870's) can also be worn as a brooch or a clasp. As you can see by the "crooked" hook, the pendant bail can be easily removed. A two piece hinge pin-stem and clasp could be inserted. The piece shown in photo **#VI-28** can be inserted across the center to transform it into a central plaque to be worn on pearls or a mesh chain. An original box has compartments for the drop and all the fittings.

VI-28; Front view.

VI-29; Back view showing where the fitting for use as a clasp can be inserted.

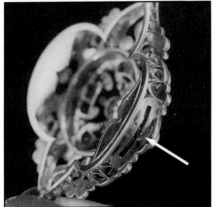

VI-30; Messada Antiques, Bond Street Antique Center, London.

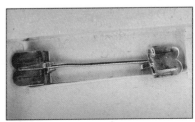

VI-31; The fitting.

This stone cameo brooch (c 1870's) converts to a pendant by inserting the tapered shank on the pendant bail into the tube that runs vertically in the back.

VI-32; 1870s Pendant Brooch. Messada Antiques, Bond Street Antique Center, London.

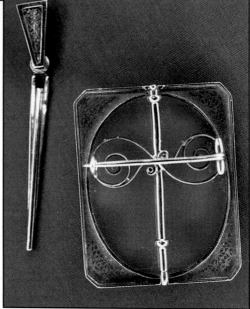

VI-33; Back of Cameo Brooch showing that the tapered stem on the bale slides behind the center rod on the back of the brooch.

Chapter VII

Testing Other Materials

This chapter will explain how to determine definitive clues for a variety of materials. These easy tests require a skill that every detective needs - that of deductive reasoning. Now don't get worried - it's not that hard. It is really just a process of elimination. By determining what the material is <u>not</u> a good detective is often lead to the right answer.

This process of elimination always makes use of our loupes and all of our built in tools. For some of the tests a "hot point" is also necessary. A home made one can be made by pushing the blunt end of a needle into the head of an eraser as shown

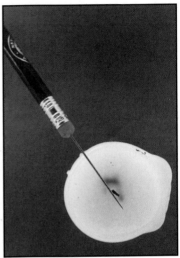

VII-1; Home-made hot point.

in photo *#VII-1*. This tool coupled with the flame from a candle can be used to test many materials. A portable, battery operated, hot point as show in photo *#VII-2* can be purchased at most jeweler's supply houses (also see the order form in the back of this book). By pressing the button on the side, the wire gets hot enough to test many materials. There will be many examples of these, later in this chapter.

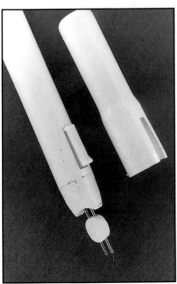

VII-2; Battery powered portable hot-point.

Black Jewelry

Many jewelry boxes, flea market and estate sales have an abundance of black pieces of jewelry. How does one know what is worth selling for 50 cents or what might be worth hundreds of dollars. Photograph **#VII-3** shows 3 pieces of black jewelry: a necklace, brooch and one earring of a pair. We already know what they are, these facts are obvious, but what are the materials? Let's go through the process that every Jewelry Detective should do to determine exactly what they are.

VII-3; *Black pendant-earring and brooch.*

The first step to valuation is identification. Let's examine the earring and see what we can find. The first tool I use is the "heft test". The earring is so light that I instantly tap it lightly against my teeth. The "click" my ears detected and the feel of it as it tapped against my teeth tells me it is probably plastic. A closer look with my loupe magnified the <u>rounded</u> <u>facet</u> <u>lines</u> that suggest plastic. Mold lines around the girdle of the "stone" confirms this. A look at the back of the earring reveals a brass ear clip. Answer - a hollow, inexpensive, plastic earring with clip backs, indicative of the 1930 - 40's.

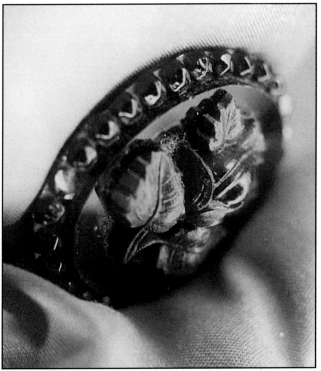

VII-4; Moulded glass leaf design joined to a flat piece of glass.

Next I pick up the black brooch. It's heft clues me in to the fact that it is not plastic or jet. The lines in the center leaves are not as crisp and well defined as you would expect in a hand carved piece. By turning the piece so that the light reflects off the surface. (See photo *#VII-4*). I am able to see a line that confirms that the flower is moulded glass joined to a flat black glass back (say that 10 times). The original pin, hinge and clasp are clues to its Victorian origin. Answer - this is a Victorian brooch made of glass with a value of approximately $100.00. If it had been jet it would have been worth at least 3 times more.

When I purchased the necklace, shown on the left in photo *#VII-3*, I assumed it was plastic. I knew from the style that it was probably made around 1910. Its heft suggested plastic or jet, but because it was not Victorian, I just assumed it was plastic. I bought it for my own pleasure so I didn't bother to test it. During my research for this book, I was testing everything. On a whim, I picked it up and rubbed it across the bottom of a piece of pottery. To my surprise it left a black mark. It was jet! The lesson I learned is <u>never</u> to <u>assume</u>. This is something we all have to deal with on a daily basis when we are wearing our Jewelry Detective hats.

Jet Test

Jet is a hard, coal-like material. It is a type of fossilized wood. The finest jet was mined in the town of Whitby, England. The industry started there in the early nineteenth century and by 1850 there were fifty jet workshops. Because it lent itself well to carving and kept a sharp edge, it was used extensively. By 1873 there were more than two hundred jet shops in this one small town.

Because jet is extremely light weight, it was the perfect material for making the enormous lockets, necklaces, brooches and bracelets that were so popular in the 1860's and 70's. The success enjoyed by the jet factories led to many imitations. French Jet which is neither French or jet (it is black glass), was cheaper to manufacture. It gave the jet industry some competition, but because it is much heavier, it was used mostly in the making of beads and smaller items.

Today, it is illegal to mine jet in Whitby. The jet is in seams in the walls of the cliffs on which parts of the town were built. Consequently, the very existence of the town was threatened by those who extracted the velvety substance. The jet cutters in the town today have to rely on the pieces that wash up on the shore of this sea cost town.

This makes the jet of the Victorian era more precious than ever. Good, well-made examples of Whitby jet are sure to appreciate in value. Recently I purchased a $900.00 jet necklace in England. I wanted it because it is almost identical to the one in photo **#VII-5**, which is on display at the Victoria and Albert Museum in London.

VII-5; Jet necklace c. 1880's. Victoria and Albert Museum.

For years to test jet pieces I would rub them on my concrete basement floor. Recently I discovered that the bottom of a piece of pottery works equally well and it is not as abrasive as concrete. Jet should always leave a black or brownish black line on the pottery. (See photo **#VII-6**) Plastic materials including Bakelite will not!

Even though jet has the "heft" of plastic, it will break. While putting on a pair of Victorian jet earrings, one slipped out of my hand and fell into the sink. The two broken pieces that I scooped into my hand left this message stamped into my mind.

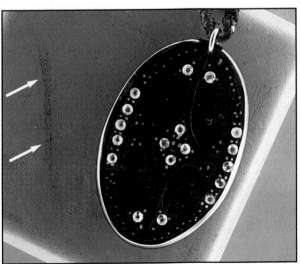

VII-6; Jet pendant necklace c. 1910. Note the black line indicating jet.

Gutta-percha

Another black or brownish material is gutta-percha. Although many of today's generation have never heard of gutta-percha, it was very prevalent during the Victorian era. Made from the sap of a Malayan tree, its usefulness was discovered during the rubber making process and introduced to England in November of 1841 The Crystal Palace Catalogue of 1851 included this definition: "The Isonandra Gutta, the source of the gum-elastic, known as gutta-percha, one of the most useful substances introduced into the arts during the present century."

Because it was very durable and highly impressionable, it lent itself well to the Victorian taste for embellishment. In its finished state it is black or brownish-black. This dark color made it a natural material for mourning jewelry, but it was by no means used exclusively for that purpose. Lockets, brooches, bracelets, and walking cane heads were but a few of its many uses.

Over 30 years ago, I bought my first piece of gutta-percha jewelry. Of course I didn't know it was gutta-percha, but I thought it was pretty even though it was dirty. After bringing it home my first job was to get the dirt out of the cracks and crevices. The cross was similar to the one in photo *#VII-7*. Not knowing what it was, I decided to use a toothbrush under a stream of hot water. I rationalized that this couldn't possibly hurt it. To my dismay it emitted a strong burnt-rubber odor. "What next", I

VII-7

thought. "Is it going to melt"? Well, it didn't melt, but it did start me on a search to find out what type of material had a rubber smelling base. This was my introduction to gutta-percha. This hot water test is still a good one to use at home.

When I'm out antiquing I have found that if you take a piece and rub it very briskly for a minute on a pants leg or coat sleeve and then hold the piece against your nose, you can small the burnt rubber odor. I usually do it on the smooth side (even the cross in photo **#VII-7** has a smooth, flat back) and try to generate enough heat with the friction to bring out the smell.

Crepe Stone

This is another black material that you may encounter. The good news is that you do not need to test it - it is glass. It is visually identifiable by its design. It's interesting that even though the patent was issued on December 25, 1883 to Fowler Brothers of Providence, Rhode Island, it was named English Crepe Stone. This was probably because anything from England was considered very "dear" to the Victorians. Some Americans still feel this way! As you can see in photo **#VII-8** it was distributed by wholesalers

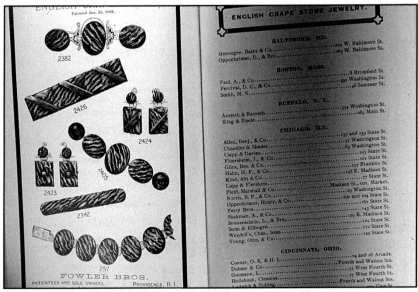

VII-8; *Fowler Brothers had distributors throughout the United States.*

across the country. This is but one page of their directory. Photo **#VII-9** shows a variety of the brooches and earrings and photo **#VII-10** shows a bracelet, stick pin and cuff link.

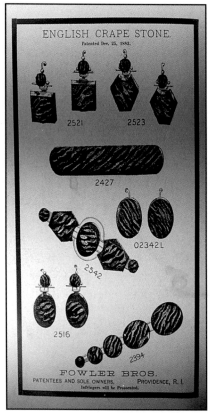

VII-9; Fowler Bros. catalogue pages.

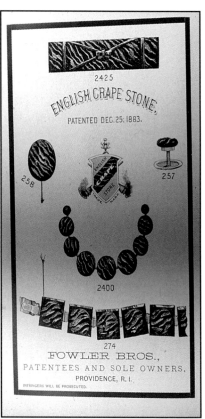

VII-10

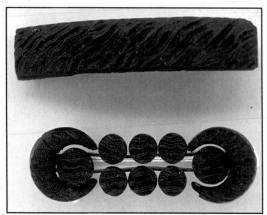

VII-11; Actual pieces of Crepe Stone Jewelry.

Photo **#VII-11** shows 2 Crepe Stone brooches. In spite of the name, I haven't found any literature that suggests that this was strictly "mourning" jewelry.

Bog Oak

Bog Oak is yet another black material. By this time you must be thinking that there are too many pieces of black jewelry. It's not that black is in the majority but that they can be so confusing. Bog Oak is exactly what it sounds as if it is. It is oak wood that has been preserved in the bogs of Ireland. Jewelry was made from it and the pieces were popular especially with tourists. The fact that Bog Oak pieces have Irish motifs makes it visually identifiable even though it is sometimes mistaken for other black materials. Photos **#VII-12, 13 & 14** show good examples of Bog Oak jewelry.

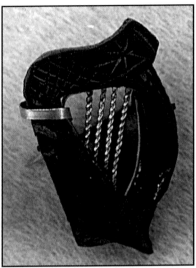

VII-12; Bog Oak Irish Harp.

VII-13; Bog Oak bracelet c.1860's with oval plaques joined by elastic threads.

VII-14; *Bog Oak Brooch.*
Note Irish motif.

Bakelite

These hinged bracelets (see photo **#VII-15**) have the "heft" of a heavy plastic. To determine what type of plastic, I put them under a stream of hot water from the kitchen sink faucet. I was checking to

VII-15; *Two Bakelite hinged bangle bracelets.*

see if I could detect the smell of varnish, formaldehyde or carbolic acid. These are the smells that most people associate with Bakelite.

Jewelry made of bakelite was popular during the 1920's and 30's. This new plastic was invented in 1909 by Leo Hendrick Bakeland (1863 - 1944). He came up with the resin while trying to develop a new type of varnish.

Bakelite is a phenolic plastic and can be moulded or cast. Jewelry items are moulded. The name Bakelite is a trade name for the Bakelite Corporation. The same mixture is known as Durez when made by the Durez Company and other names when manufactured by other companies.

Another test for Bakelite can be done by putting 409 bathroom cleaner on a cotton swab. I chose a place on the inside of each bracelet. By rubbing gently for a minute (I twirl the cotton end around a small area) you should be able to detect a very faint to a bright yellow color. The swabs I used on the bracelets are pictured in photo *#VII-17*.

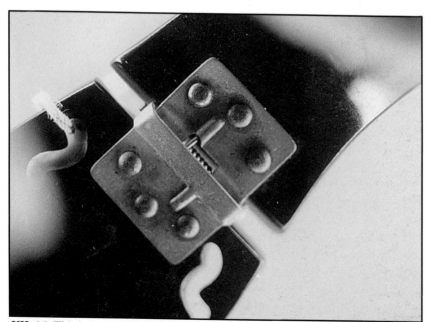

VII-16; *This is the type hinge that is on the bangle bracelets on the opposite page. The quality of this hinge and the way it's attached is indicative of the quality that went in to much of the Bakelite Jewelry.*

VII-16; The yellow on the Q-tips is a sure sign of "Bakelite". This one was used to test a bracelet pictured on the previous page.

Ivory

Ivory, one of the oldest materials used for ornamental purposes, has been recognized throughout the history of civilization for its beauty and value. As most people know, Ivory is the tusk of the African Elephant. But many do not realize that the tusks of the hippopotamus and walrus are also classified as ivory. Elephant ivory is distinguishable by its "cross hatched" or "engine turned" look when viewed under magnification. (see illustration *#VII-18 & 19*).

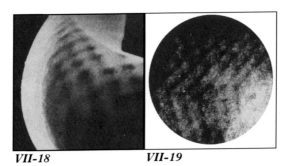

VII-18   *VII-19*

Cross hatched look of Ivory under magnification. Photos courtesy of the Gemological Institute of America.

The other ivories have wavy grain lines. Once the ivory has been carved into bracelets, necklaces, and ear-rings, it is very hard to distinguish its origin.

Photo *#VII-20* shows a brooch and a necklace pendent. A tiny prick with my hot point needle told me that the brooch was plastic by the way it easily melted around the head of the needle. The hot point didn't leave a mark on the necklaces. I did another test using the nitric acid from my gold testing kit. A tiny drop of this solution in an inconspicuous place started the acid to effervesce. These tiny clear bubbles were proof that the pendant was animal ivory. Many

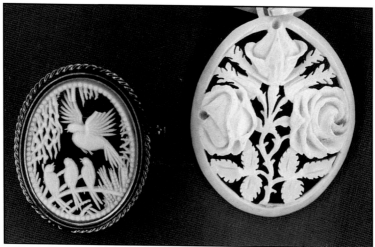

VII-20; Plastic or Ivory?

pieces of carved ivory have been coated with a waxy finish and it is sometimes difficult to find a place that will react to the acid. I always look for a tiny crack in which to deposit my acid. This usually does the trick.

The so-called vegetable ivories, the coroze nut from South America and the doum-palm nut from Central Africa, are often mistaken for genuine ivory. They are used to make beads and smaller items. When tested with nitric acid, these pieces turn a rosy color.

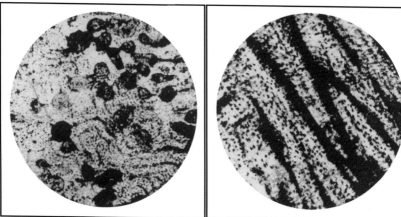

VII-21; Bone magnified 25 times.

VII-22; Longitude section magnified 50 times.

Bone is also used to imitate ivory. It has a dryer and coarser look than ivory. The photos of bone magnified 25 to 50 times in photo **#VII-21 & 22** (Courtesy of Gemological Institute of America). show this coarser look.

Don't try to clean or bleach your ivory pieces. Ivory tends to yellow with age, but this only adds to its beauty and value. As you read this paragraph there are a multitude of people in China soaking ivory with tea and other mixtures to make it look old.

Never subject ivory to extreme temperature change. This can cause splitting and cracking. Ivory is also porous so be sure to keep it away from anything that might discolor it.

Coral

VII-23; Which pieces are coral? Read on!

The group of jewelry in photo **#VII-23** looks as if it could be a group of coral jewelry. Not true!

Coral is the calcareous skeletons of marine animals. It is found in abundance in the Naples area. The most prized colors are deep red and angel skin pink. Because coral is easy to work, it is used

for designs which call for a profusion of flowers and leaves.
The Victorians had a special love for coral jewelry. Since Roman
times it was believed to possess the power to ward off evil and
danger. Consequently, it was a favorite Victorian christening
present.

Coral was not limited to the young. In 1845 the Prince of the Two
Sicilies gave his bride, the Duchess d' Aumale, a beautiful parue of
coral jewelry. This started a fashion among women of all ages that
continued to the late 1860's.

In the 1920's coral became popular again. Any time the color coral
is in vogue so is coral jewelry. Some of the most fashionable pieces
this spring and summer are made of coral.

While genuine coral comes in a variety of shades and tints, the
only true piece of coral in the group picture is the branch coral
necklace (the second one from the left). The necklace on the far
right has moulded roses. It is the one we discussed in Chapter I.
The necklace on the far left is dyed bone and the center necklace
is plastic. The dress clip between the two plastic necklaces is
embellished with glass cabochons of "coral" and "coral" flowers
made of celluloid.

True coral is much heavier than its imitations. It also effervesces
when touched with nitric acid.

Celluloid

Celluloid was the trade name given to this material by its inventor,
John Wesley Hyatt in 1869. It was widely used in the 1890 - 1920's
time period. Celluloid is a man-made plastic consisting of a
mixture of pyroxylin and camphor and it was used to imitate
tortoise, ivory and coral. Its flammability proved its downfall and
eventually it was taken off the market for safety reasons. The
brooch clip in photo **#VII-23** on the opposite page circa 1930's is
a late use of celluloid.

When testing plastic one must be extra careful to touch the pieces
with the hot point <u>away</u> from the nose. Celluloid is highly

flammable. Although I have never experienced a nose-burn, please do not take a chance. Celluloid will often make a sizzling sound and will always emit the odor of camphor. If you do not know what camphor smells like, go to the drug store and purchase a bottle of camphorated oil.

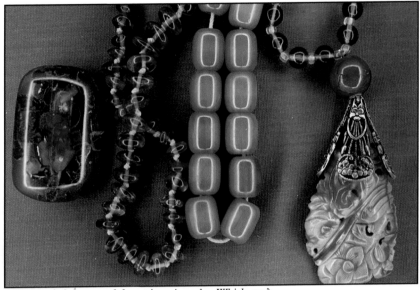

VII-24; *At least one of these pieces is amber. Which one?*

Amber

The 4 pieces pictured in photo ***#VII-24*** all appear to be amber. But a good detective knows that things aren't always what they appear to be.

Amber is fossilized tree resin. Over fifty million years ago trees taller than the Redwoods of today grew along the shore of the Baltic Sea. The Glacier Age caused them to be swept into the sea. There they solidified under ice and pressure. Scientists believe that the trees probably had a fungus of some type because the resin was so loose it even surrounded dew drops. Consequently, amber often has insects, petals of flowers, seeds and bark locked inside. These add to the value of the gem.

Although light yellow (honey colored) is the color most associated with the name, it can be a variety of shades of yellow, brown or even red (cherry amber). Color varies according to the depth of water into which the tree fell. Amber can be translucent, opaque, or a mixture of both.

The Greeks called amber "lectron", which is the root word for electricity. This electrical property was probably one of the first test used for amber. Take a few small bits of tissue (in olden days they used straw) and put it on a table. Rub the article in question briskly against woolen or cotton cloth and then immediately place it in front of the bits of tissue. True amber will make the tissue move. Unfortunately, some of today's plastics will do the same thing.

Another test is done by sticking a hot needle into an inconspicuous spot on the amber. If the piece is genuine, it will emit a pine-like odor. But, this test is not always conclusive because artificial amber made in Russia includes small bits of genuine amber. If the needle should hit any of these pieces, it would smell authentic.

The only true test is done with ether. Place a small amount on a cotton swab and apply it to the piece in questions (in an inconspicuous place of course). If the piece is genuine, the ether will not affect it. If it is plastic, it will become sticky and the ether will eat into it. I acquired my ether through my doctor but I've only had to use it once in the last 10 years.

Amber has a very distinctive "feel". Most people are shocked at how "light" it is. They can't believe that the large piece that they are holding can weigh so little.
Visit as many places as possible that have amber for sale. With time and practice you should eventually be able to spot a good piece through visual identification.

In photo **#VII-24**, the necklace made of irregular amber pieces (second piece from the left) is the only genuine piece. The brooch on the left is plastic with small pieces of included amber. The beads test plastic and the pendant is bakelite.

VII-254A; Side view showing mould marks on the plastic disc.   *VII-25B; Left to right: plastic necklace, tortoise shell necklace and tortoise shell turtle.*

Tortoise Shell

Two of the items in Photo *#VII-24* are tortoise and one is a plastic imitation. Can you guess which is which?

Tortoise comes form the hawksbill turtle. Even though this is the smallest of marine turtles, it usually weights between one hundred and two hundred pounds. Both the mottled upper shell and the lower "yellow belly" are used for ornamental purposes.

Tortoise shell is one of nature's natural plastics. It can be heated and moulded or cut into many forms. Unfortunately, celluloid can imitate it well enough to fool the human eye. So how does one know if the beautiful antique hair comb is plastic or tortoise? A simple test can tell. One touch with a hot needle is usually enough to emit the strong odor of burning hair. If you do not know what hair smells like cut a small piece of your hair and burn it. Chances are that you will never forget the odor.

As for the items in photo *#VII-25B*, the turtle is tortoise and so is the inlaid necklace. The necklace on the far left is plastic. Photo *#VIII-25A* shows the tell-tale mould line.

In Victorian times Pique was popular for jewelry. For Pique jewelry the tortoise shell is heated and a design is formed (star, cross, etc.). Into this design "dots" or "racks" are drilled. Pique is the French word for points. These minute spaces are inlaid with silver or gold rods. The hot tortoise shell emits a glue-like film which, along with the natural contraction caused by the cooling of the shell, snugly seals the metal.

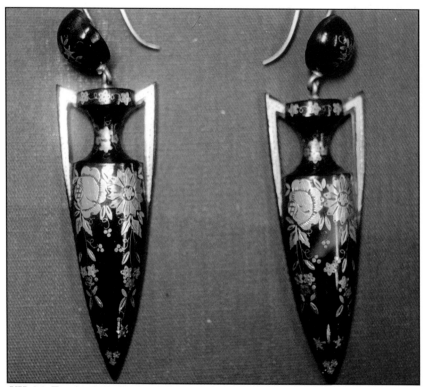

VII-26; Tortoise shell pique earrings in a Grecian urn design. Sue Brown Antiques, London. $2,530

Many lovely pieces were made using this process. Pique has been in and out of fashion since the sixteenth century. In the nineteenth century it was popular during 1820's and the 1870's. Today it is highly collectible. When a piece comes on the market it is quickly purchased by a collector. Since Pique is not being reproduced, it most assuredly will continue to appreciate in value.

Mosaics

Mosaic and the materials of which they are made are things that a good Jewelry Detective should be familiar. The basic types of mosaics associated with jewelry are Pietra Dura, Venetian and Roman.

The mosaics from Florence are commonly known as "pietra dura" (hard stone). These works of art are made by cutting designs out of stones much as malachite and carnelian, and fitting them together in a black background. This was done

VII-27; Pietra Dura pendant. Sue Brown Antiques, Davis Muse, London.

so expertly that magnifying glass is needed to verify that the design is indeed made from pieces and not painted. Flowers and birds were favorite motifs. Photo *#VII-27* is of a Pietra Dura pendant circa 1860's - 80's with a compartment for hair in the back.

VII-28; Turning a mosaic so that the light will reflect off the surface will enable you to see the tiny pieces that make up the design.

VII-29; Venetian mosaic pin c. early 1900's.

Venetian mosaics are not made of natural stone. Instead the designs are made by shaping different colored pieces of glass and inlaying them to create the desired pattern. You can see by Photos **#VII-28** & **29** that the quality of mosaics varies. The brooch plaque shown in photo **#VII-28** is from the mid 1800's. The pin in photo **#VII-29** is from the early 1900's.

Roman mosaics are made of tiny rectangular bricks of glass. In the early 1700's, the Vatican was already making these pieces to sell to visitors. The motifs are typical Roman ruins and other familiar scenes of Rome. Many designs were taken from mosaics found in the ruins of Pompeii. Again a magnifying glass is needed to fully appreciate the craftsmanship that went into creating these souvenir pieces.

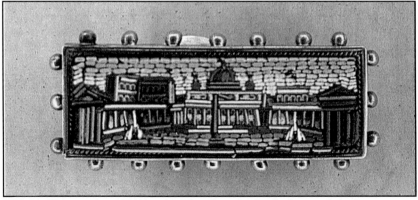

VII-30; This mosaic c.1880' is enlarged to show the details. Its actual size is approximately 1-1/4" x 5/8". Very small, but from that perspective it looks like a painted scene.

Seed Pearl Jewelry

Jewelry made of tiny seed pearls is another lost art with which most people are not familiar. A seed pearl weighs less than 1/4 of a grain. Seed pearl jewelry was made by threading a multitude of these tiny pearls on white horse hair to form the desired pattern. After this was completed it was attached by white horse hair to a mother of pearl backing that had been cut for the piece.

This type of jewelry was popular from the late 1700's through the mid 1800's. Because many people do not know about this jewelry you can still sometimes find it at bargain prices. I found a beautiful pair of earrings in an antique shop in Orlando, Florida in January 2000 for only $12.00. Photos *#VII-31 & 32* show the front and back of a seed pearl brooch. The brooch and earrings in picture *#VII-33* originally belonged to Martha Washington.

VII-31; Seed pearl brooch.

VII-32; Back view showing how the pearls are attached to the mother of pearl backing.

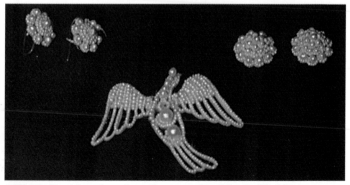

VII-33; Pearl brooch and earrings owned by Martha Washington. Mount Vernon Museum.

Paintings on Porcelain

The paintings on porcelain that were worn throughout the 19th century, probably evolved out of the popularity of the portrait miniatures of the 18th century.

Portraits of women on porcelain are the most popular. The Romanticism of the Victorian period brought portraits of characters from literature painted on porcelain into vogue.

In the latter part of the 19th century, the painting of flowers on porcelain was a ladies pastime. These are usually identifiable by the gold painted rim around the porcelain and the one piece pin assembly that is always glued on.

Transfers have been around for over 200 years. This process allows a printed picture to be transferred to a surface giving the impression that it has been hand painted. Many "paintings on porcelain" are in reality just transfers. Some of the transfers were augmented with paint and complete with brush strokes.

Fortunately for us Jewelry Detectives the process used in printing the transfers leave tiny little dots that can be detected with a loupe. Always examine the painting carefully. The value is never as great for a transfer as for a hand painted piece.

Photo **#VII-34** is of "The Vagabond Boy" (c.1860's - 80's) set in a jet plaque, all hand painted.

VII-34; Hand painted vagabond boy.

The lovely lady in photo **#VII-35** is a transfer augmented with brush strokes. Only by closely examining her face can you detect the tale-tale dots indicative of a transfer.

VII-35; A transfer on porcelain augmented with brush stokes.

Butterfly Wings

Some unusual materials have often found their way into jewelry. A butterfly wing is such a material. Popular from the late 1800's through the 1940's, they made use of the iridescent blue wings as a background for pendants, brooches, earrings and rings. They often included hand painted caribbean scenes. Photo **#VII-36** shows a sterling pendant with a painted butterfly wing under domed glass. The rectangles of white that is visible on the glass is a reflection from the light. For more pictures and prices on Butterfly Jewelry see <u>Answers and Questions about Old Jewelry</u> 1840 - 1950. Butterfly Wing jewelry is visually identifiable.

VII-36; If you look carefully you can see a palm tree and water painted on the background of a butterfly wing.

Shell Cameos

Cameo's have been carved out of shell for hundreds of years. They are still popular today. Unfortunately there are some excellent composition cameo's on the market. With practice, shell cameo's can be visually identified. If you have a gold test kit a drop of the nitric acid will detect a shell cameo in an instant. Shells effervesce (bubbles up)

VII-37; A shell cameo c.1920.

when a drop of acid is placed on its underside. The acid will not damage the cameo. Composition cameo's will not react to the nitric acid. My famous teeth test will also separate composition cameos from shell cameos.

Aurora Borealis

This trade name is used for glass or plastic that has been coated with a compound to give it an iridescent look. It was popular in the 1950s & 60's and is still made today. Because it is visually identifiable a picture is worth a thousand words.

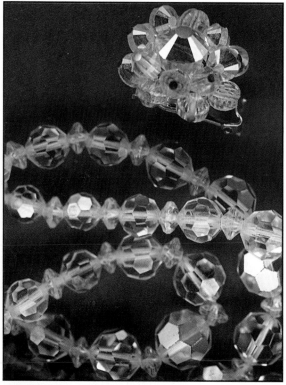

VII-38; Aurora Borealis glass beads.

Beetle Jewelry

No, I don't mean jewelry commemorating "THE BEATLES". This ugly beetle was revered by the Egyptians as a symbol of good fortune and everlasting life. These beetles buried their eggs in dung and dirt. When the Egyptians saw them hatch out of the ground they became the Egyptian symbol of rebirth.

These scarabs were also used as seals. The Egyptians made beetle ornaments from real beetles, clay, glass and stone.

There have been several Egyptian revival periods in the last 150 years. With each revival, Egyptian motifs of all types came back into vogue. But jewelry made from real beetles is one of the most unusual. They were set in base metals and precious materials. The Smithsonian Institution has some beautiful examples of gold jewelry c.1860 set with real beetles.

The necklace in photo *#VII-39* is circa 1920's and set in gold over brass. I believe it was originally longer than it is now. It was probably shortened when style dictated a shorter length. Stone scarab jewelry is very popular again today.

VII-39; Beetle necklace. Private collection of Shirley Swabb, Philadelphia, PA.

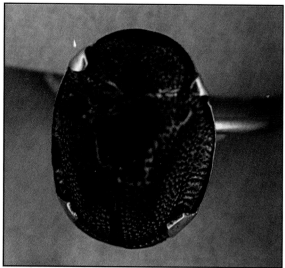

VII-40; Beetle ring. Note the iridescence.

Smells Tell

Below is a list of several materials and their identifying odors. Always remember to stick the hot needle into an inconspicuous place:

Amber: Pine scent when heated with a hot point.

Bakelite: Carbolic acid when placed under hot tap water.

Celluloid: Camphor when heated with a hot point.

Jet: Burning coal when heated with a hot point.

Tortoise Shell: Burning hair when heated with a hot point.

Gutta Percha: Burning rubber smell when placed under hot tap water.

Chapter VIII

Test Yourself
Solve the Mysteries

The information in this book will not do you any good unless you put it to the "test". These simple cases will give you an opportunity to flex your "Jewelry Detective" brain waves.

Take a deep breath, relax and let the "juices" flow. This is an open book exam so don't hesitate to look up anything that gives you a problem.

Is your paper and pen ready? Go!!!

Case #1 - "Case of the U.S.O.'s"
(Unidentified Stationary Objects)

In photo *#VIII-1* & *VIII-2* *(next page)*, we have 2 unidentified objects. Your mission, if you choose to accept, is to identify what the two pieces are; from what materials they are made; and, which is the older piece. Please list all the clues that lead you to your conclusions.

VIII-1; *Two brooches. What are they made of?*

VIII-2; Note the clasps and hinges.

Case #2 - "What's Wrong"?

Photo *#VIII-3* shows the backs of a brooch and earrings c.1860's. The fronts are Roman Mosaics depicting Roman Ruins. Your mission is to look at the earrings and brooch and determine what is wrong in this picture. Can you also give a clue or two that leads you to your conclusions.

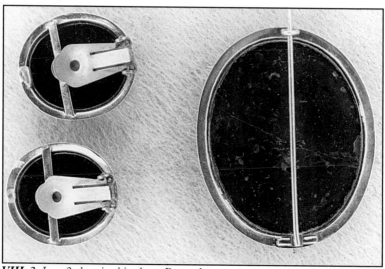

VIII-3; I see 2 clues in this photo. Do you?

Case #3 - "What's in a Name"?

In this case we know that one suspect bears the name Hattie
Carnegie and the other Eisenberg. Can you determine the more
valuable of the two? Don't just guess. Please give reasons for your
brilliant deductions. Which piece is older and how did you detect
it? Use photos **#*VIII-4, 5, 6*, *7* and *8*.**

VIII-4   *VIII-5*

VIII-6   *VIII-7*

VIII-8

Case #4 - "The Bookchain Mystery"

This bookchain necklace is circa 1860 - 80. It appears to be multi-colored gold. Is it? I have taken the liberty of dropping a touch of acid on the underside of one of the links. Look for the reaction on the left hand side of photo **#VIII-9B** which is a close up of the link. What clues does the acid uncover? What is the metal?

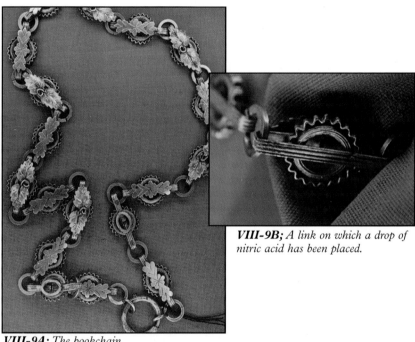

VIII-9B; A link on which a drop of nitric acid has been placed.

VIII-9A; The bookchain.

Case #5 - "The Case of the Missing Stem"

Photo **#VIII-10** is the back side of a lavalier circa 1890 - 1900. It is stamped 18 ct. Does it have fittings or findings. What is its country of origin?

VIII-10; What clue tells you the country of origin of this lavalier/brooch combination.

Case #6 - "All that Glitters"

Photo **#VIII-11** pictures some glittery pieces of jewelry. Are any of the pieces set with diamonds? If so, which ones? How did you come to your conclusion?

VIII-11; *Two necklaces, a brooch and a watchband.*

VIII-12; *Back view.*

VIII-13; *Close-up of the stones and necklace.*

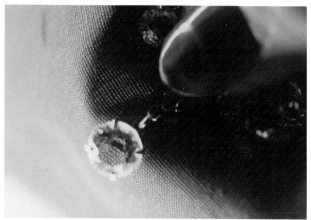

VIII-14; *What do you see?*

Case #7 - "Truth and Consequences"

An elderly rich lady called to say that a few years ago a lady had done a good deed for her. She didn't know the identity of the lady but the person had accidentally left behind a plain silver colored band. She wanted the Jewelry Detective to find its owner so that she could generously reward her for her kindness.

The Jewelry Detective placed an advertisement in the newspaper explaining the situation and asking the owner of a plain silver colored ring to come forward. The ring's only identifying mark was a mark stamped on the inside of the band. (See illustration **#VIII-A**.)

VIII-A

The first caller said that the ring was given to her by her great-grandmother and she had no idea that she had left it behind.

The next caller explained that she had purchased the ring in England about 20 years ago. It was a souvenir of her trip and she had wondered what had happened to it.

A woman with an English accent answered the advertisement and explained that the ring had been her mother's wedding band when she had married in the 1930's. The caller had been on vacation in the United States when she encountered the elderly lady and had probably taken it off when she had washed her hands.

All three of the callers were anxious to pick up their ring and their generous reward. As the Jewelry Detective, who would you give it to and why?

Case #8 -
"The Case of the Black Abbey Ruins"

Photo **#VIII-15** shows a brooch embellished with a carving of the ruins of an ancient building. What is its country of origin? What is it made of?

VIII-15; The mysterious black brooch c.1860's.

Case #9 –
"The Case of the Red Necklace"

A client comes into your Jewelry Detective Agency with the pendant necklace pictured in photo **#VII16A & B**. It belonged to someone in their family, but she did not know if it was her mother's (born 1919) or her grandmother's (born 1894). Could we help her to date it and tell her anything about it?

Clue #1: The heft of the piece indicates plastic.

Clue #2: The teeth test indicates plastic.

Clue #3: The long black ribbon with a slide attachment could indicate a piece from 1910 - 20's.

Clue #4: Because the piece is set with red stones it was not feasible to put it under hot water and do a "smell test", so we start by using a hot point. When the hot point was placed on the back of the slide inside the opening for the ribbon, there was a sizzle sound, a puff of smoke and the smell of camphor. What did that test tell us about the age of the piece and the material it was made of? Was it purchased as new by the mother or the grandmother?

VIII-16A; *Was it the mother's?*   **VIII-16B;** *Or the grandmother's*

Case #10 - What's in a Name II"?

The shrill ring of the telephone awakened me from a deep dream. "Hello" I answered in a sleepy voice. "I need your help" said a female voice on the other end of the line. I just purchased a necklace at a flea market and the dealer didn't know a thing about it except that she had bought it from the estate of an old lady."

"I don't' know how much help I can give you over the telephone, but maybe if you hold it really close to the receiver, it might help." I replied still feeling resentful about having my treasure hunting dream interrupted.

"What does it look like?" I asked.

"The pendant drop is a butterfly made of a material that may be plastic. It's a yellow orange color and very light weight." She answered.

"Does it have any markings on it?"

"I haven't really looked" she said, "give me a minute. It looks like the letters GIP are engraved into the back of the material. Can you tell me <u>anything</u> about it?" I can, can you?

Knowing this bit of information, you should be able to tell her what the piece is made of and who made it.

Finished? I just know that you're a great Jewelry Detective! If you are not so sure, just log on to the Jewelry Box Antiques website: <u>www.jewelryboxantiques.com</u> and click on the Jewelry Detective page. The answers are awaiting you.

Bonus Pictures

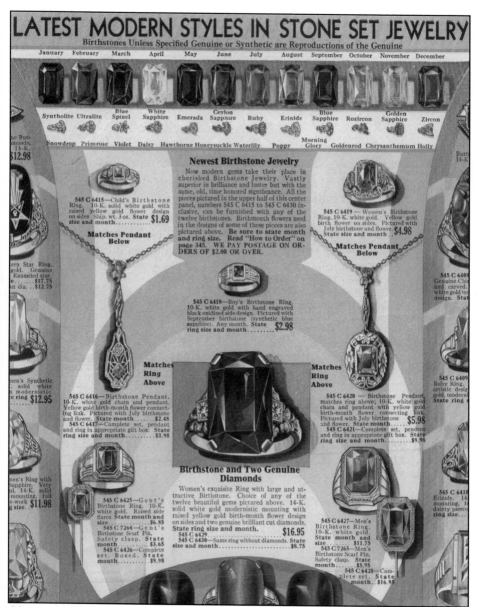

Montgomery Wards Catalogue 1931-32. Read the line underneath the "heading" very carefully.

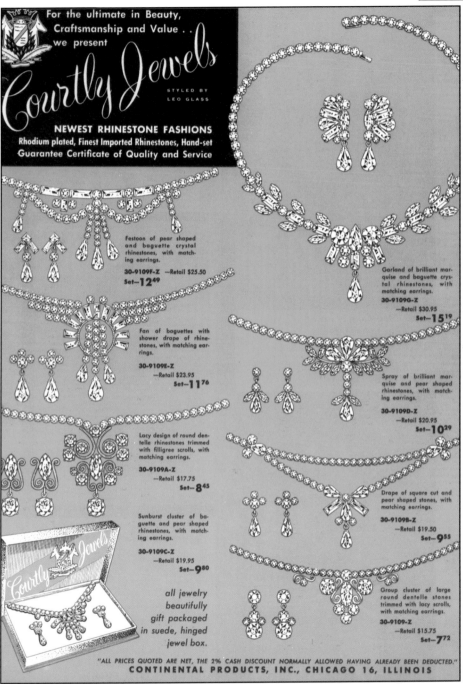

For the ultimate in Beauty, Craftsmanship and Value .. we present

Courtly Jewels

STYLED BY
LEO GLASS

NEWEST RHINESTONE FASHIONS
Rhodium plated, Finest Imported Rhinestones, Hand-set
Guarantee Certificate of Quality and Service

Festoon of pear shaped and baguette crystal rhinestones, with matching earrings.
30-9109F-Z —Retail $25.50
Set—12⁴⁹

Fan of baguettes with shower drape of rhinestones, with matching earrings.
30-9109E-Z —Retail $23.95
Set—11⁷⁶

Lacy design of round dentelle rhinestones trimmed with filligree scrolls, with matching earrings.
30-9109A-Z —Retail $17.75
Set—8⁴⁵

Sunburst cluster of baguette and pear shaped rhinestones, with matching earrings.
30-9109C-Z —Retail $19.95
Set—9⁸⁰

all jewelry beautifully gift packaged in suede, hinged jewel box.

Garland of brilliant marquise and baguette crystal rhinestones, with matching earrings.
30-9109G-Z —Retail $30.95
Set—15¹⁹

Spray of brilliant marquise and pear shaped rhinestones, with matching earrings.
30-9109D-Z —Retail $20.95
Set—10²⁹

Drape of square cut and pear shaped stones, with matching earrings.
30-9109B-Z —Retail $19.50
Set—9⁵⁵

Group cluster of large round dentelle stones trimmed with lacy scrolls, with matching earrings.
30-9109-Z —Retail $15.75
Set—7⁷²

"ALL PRICES QUOTED ARE NET, THE 2% CASH DISCOUNT NORMALLY ALLOWED HAVING ALREADY BEEN DEDUCTED."
CONTINENTAL PRODUCTS, INC., CHICAGO 16, ILLINOIS

These courtly jewels are by Leo Glass. Look him up in the Maker's Mark section under costume jewelry. This is a Continental Prod. Inc. catalogue, Chicago, IL, 1951-52 issue. Note the wholesale and retail prices. They were not cheap! Remember a loaf of bread was only .15 cents.

Cameo carved out of lava from Mt.
Vesuvius c. 1840-50's.

Rolled gold plate beauty pins. Today
these would be called gold filled.

Full view of the vermeil "Jelly Belly". Did
you look up the design patent date?

Bakelite Jewelry on display at the Smithsonian Institution's American History Museum.

A color shot showing wear points on a gold over brass piece. Unfortunately they're not all this easy to see.

Color picture of the back of a dress clip showing the gold foiled backing on the rhinestones.

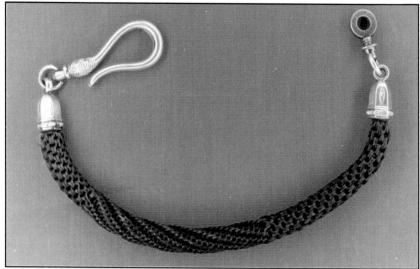

Hairwork watchchain c.1940's. This was woven on a work-table.

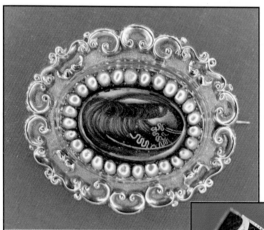

Brooch containing a pallet-worked piece of hair worked into a curl, mid 1800's.

Hinge bangle bracelet with table-worked hair. Hair is visually identifiable with practice.

BIBLIOGRAPHY, RESOURCES & RECOMMENDED READING

Armstrong, Mary. *Victorian Jewelry*,
New York: McMillian Publishing Co., 1976. A beautiful book about jewelry.

Becker, Vivienne. *Antique & Twentieth Century Jewellery.*
Second Edition, N.A. G. Press Ltd., 1922.

Bell, Jeanenne. *Answers to Questions About Old Jewelry 1840 - 1950.*
Fifth Edition, Iola, WI: Krause Publications, 1999.

Beuer, J. and A. *A Book of Jewels*, Prague: Artia, 1966.

Bradbury, Frederich. *Bradbury's Book of Hallmarks*,
Sheffield, England: J. W. Northend Ltd., 1928.

Bradford, Ernie. *English Victorian Jewellery*,
New York: Robert M. McBrode & Co. Inc., 1957.

Bradford, Ernie. *Four Centuries of European Jewellery*,
Great Britain: Spring Books, 1967.

Brenda, Klement. *Ornament and Jewellery*,
Pragues Svoboda, 1967. Archeological finds from Eastern Europe.

Burgess, Frederich W. *Antique Jewelry and Trinkets*,
New York: Tudor Publishing Co., 1919.

Bury, Shirley. *Jewellery 1789 - 1910*, Vol. I and Vol. II,
Great Britain, Antique Collectors Club 1991.

Cera, Deanna Fareti. *Costume Jewellery*,
Great Brittain, Antique Collectors Club 1997.

Curran, Mona. *A Treasury of Jewels and Gems*,
New York: Emerson Books Inc., 1962.

Curran, Mona. *Collecting Antique Jewellery*,
New York: Emerson Books Inc., 1964

Dietz, Joselit, Smead, Zapata. *The Glitter and the Gold*,
USA: The Newark Museum, 1997.

Dolan, Maryanne. *Collecting Rhinestone and Colored Jewelry*,
Iola, WI: Krause Publications, 1998.

Evans, Joan. *A History of Jewellery 1100 - 1870*,
Boston, Mass.: Boston Book and Art Publications, 1970.

Flower, Margaret. *Victorian Jewellery*,
New York: Duell, Sloan and Pearce, 1951.

Fregnac, Claude. *Jewellery From The Renaissance to Art Nouveau*,
London: Octopus Books, 1973.

Gene, Charlotte. *Victorian Jewelry Design*,
Chicago: Henery Regnery Co., 1973.

Giltay-Nijseen L. *Jewelry New York*: Universe Books, 1964.

Goldemberg, Rose Leeman. *Antique Jewelry, A Practical and
Passionate Guide*, New York: Crown Publishers, 1976.

Hornung, Clarence P. *Antique and Jewelry Designs*,
New York: George Braziller, 1968.

Jessup, Ronald. *Anglo-Saxon Jewellery*,
United Kingdom: Shire Publishers Ltd., 1974.

Jewelry Ancient to Modern, New York: Viking Press in cooperation
with the Walters Art Gallery, Baltimore, 1979.

Kuzel, Vladislav. *A Book of Jewelry*, Prague: Artia, 1962.

Liddicoat, Richard. *The Jeweler's Manual*,
CA: Gemological Institute of America, 1974.

Matlins, Antoinette and A.C. Bonanno. *Gem Identification Made Easy*,
Woodstock, Vermont: Gemstone Press, 1997.

McNeil, Donald S. *Jewelers Dictionary*, Radnor, PA: 1976.

Miller, Anna M. *Cameo's Old & New*, Von Nostrand Rhinhold, 1991.

Morrill, Penny and Carole Berk. *Mexican Silver*,
PA: Schiffer Publications 1994.

Parry, Karina. *Bakelite Bangles*, Iola, WI: Krause Publications, 1999.

Percival, MacIver. *Chats on Old Jewellery and Trinkets*,
New York: Frederich A. Stokes Co., 1902.

Peter, Mary. *Collecting Victorian Jewellery*,
New York: Emerson Books, Inc., 1971.

Phillips, Clare. *Jewelry From Antiquity to the Present*,
London: Thames and Hudson, 1996.

Romero, Christie. *Warman's Jewelry*.
Second Edition, Iola, WI: Krause Publications, 1999.

Sataloff, Joseph and Alison Richards, *The Pleasures of Jewelry &
Gemstones*, London: Octopus Books, 1975. A beautifully
informative book.

Schumann, Walter. *Gemstones of the World*,
New York: Sterling Publishing Co., 1979. A great book
on gemstones.

Smith, H. Clifford. *Jewellery*, New York: G.P. Putnam & Co., 1908.

Tolkin, Tracy and Henrietta Wilkerson. *A Collector's Guide to Costume Jewelry*, Canada: Firefly Books, 1997.

TradeMarks of the Jewelry and Kindred Trades, New York: The Jewelers Circular Keystone Publication Co., 1915.

Wyler, Seymour B. *The Book of Old Silver*, New York: Crown Publishing Inc., 1937.

RESOURCES

EDUCATIONAL RESOURCES

1. **G.I.A.** - The world's largest non-profit educational organization for the jewelry industry.
   Gemological Institute of America
   5345 Armada Drive
   Carlsbad, CA 92008
   General Info: (760) 603-4200
   Course Info: (800) 366-8519

2. **College of Appraisers** - Courses in all phases of antiques, including jewelry.
   120 So. Bradford Avenue
   Placontia, CA 92870

3. **Hairwork Society**
   P. O. Box 806
   Pleasant Grove, Utah 84062
   (801) 785-7210

4. **American Society of Jewelry Historians**
   1333A North Avenue, Box 103
   New Rochelle, NY 10804
   (914) 637-0087

5. **Antiques Dealers & Collectors Association** - A great association. Lots of educational opportunities. Membership only $35.00 yearly.
   P.O. Box 2782
   Huntsville, NC 28070
   1-800-287-7127

APPRAISAL ORGANIZATIONS

A call to these organizations will yield a list of appraisers in your area that includes experts in jewelry and gemstones.

1. **International Society of Appraisers**
   16040 Christensen Road
   Suite 120
   Seattle, WA 98188
   (888) 472-4732

2. **National Association of Jewelry Appraisers**
   P. O. Box 6558
   Annapolis, MD 21401-0558
   (301) 261-8270

3. **Channelspace.com** - On line appraisals - live Web broadcast entertainment. www.collectingchannel.com

Shows such as The Antiques Roadshow, Treasures In Your Home and the collectible and appraisal shows on the Home & Garden Channel sometimes offer good jewelry clues.

Look for these exciting additions to the Antiques Detectives "**How to**" series:

The Doll Detective
The Pottery Detective
The Stamp Detective
The Pocketwatch Detective
The Oriental Rug Detective
The American Indian Jewelry Detective

The Glass Detective
The Furniture Detective
The Silver Detective
The Antique Toy Detective
The Coin Detective

7325 Quivira Rd. #238
Shawnee, Kansas 66216
Phone: 913-962-8533
Fax: 913-962-4418

GLOSSARY

A

Albert Chain: A watch chain for a man or a woman with a bar at one end and a swivel to hold a watch at the other.

Algrette: Jewels mounted in a shape resembling feathers or a feather motif.

A-jour Setting: An open work setting in which the bottom portion of the stone can be seen. Also a setting in which the metal has open work.

Alloy: A metal made by combining 2 or more metals to make the resulting metal a different color or fineness.

Assaying: chemically testing a precious metal to determine its purity.

B

Baguette: A stone in the shape of a narrow rectangle.

Banded Agate: Agate which has bands of lighter and darker colors. It can be onyx (black/white), cornelian (orangish red/white), or sardonyx (brown/white).

Bangle: A rigid bracelet often tubular and hinged.

Baton: A stone cut in the shape of a long narrow rectangle.

Bead Set: Used to define a setting in which stones are held into place by small balls or beads of metal.

Belcher Mounting: A claw type ring mounting of which there were many variations. Popular from the 1870's thru 1920's.

Bezel: A metal rim which holds the stone in a ring, a cameo in its mounting or a crystal on a watch.

Black Amber: A misnomer for jet.

Bog Oak: Wood preserved in the bogs of Ireland and used to make jewelry during the Victorian era.

Bohemian Garnet: A dark red pyrope garnet.

Brilliant Cut: A cut that returns the greatest amount of white light to the eye. It usually has 57 or 58 facets. Used for diamonds and other transparent stones.

Briolettes: A teardrop-shaped cut covered with facets.

Brooch: An ornamental piece of jewelry which has a pin back for affixing it to clothing or hats. Usually larger in scale than the ones referred to as "pins".

C

Cabochon: A stone cut in a round or oval shape in which the top is convex shaped (not faceted).

Calibre Cut: Small stones cut in the shape of squares, rectangles or oblongs and calibrated to fit the mounting.

Cameo: A layered stone in which a design is engraved on the top layer and the remainder is carved away to reveal the next layer, leaving the design in relief. Also done in shell, coral, lava and all types of gemstones.

Cameo Habille: A type of cameo in which the carved head is adorned with a necklace, earrings or head ornament set with small stones.

Carat: A unit of weight for gemstones. Since 1913 one metric carat is one fifth of a gram or 200 milligrams.

Carbuncle: Today used to refer to a garnet cut in cabochon. In the middle ages it referred to any cabochon cut red stone.

Cartouche: An ornamental tablet used in decoration or to be engraved, usually symmetrical.

Celluloid: One of the first plastics. A compound of camphor and gun cotton. Highly flammable.

Channel Setting: A type of setting in which stones of the same size are held in place by a continuous strip of metal at the top and bottom literally creating a channel for the stones.

Chasing: The technique of embellishing metal by hand using hammers and punches to make indentations; thus raising the design.

Chaton: The central or main ornament of a ring.

Cipher: A monogram of letters intertwined.

Claw Setting: A style of ring setting in which the stone is held by a series of vertically projecting prongs.

Clip: A piece of jewelry resembling a brooch but instead of having a pin stem to fasten into clothing it has a hinged clip that hooks over and into the fabric. Very popular from the 1920s-40's. Sometimes made into a brooch that incorporated a double clip. It could be worn as a brooch or disassembled and used as a pair of clips.

Coin Silver: a term used for metal with a 90% silver content and 10% copper. This was the same fineness of American silver coins.

Collet Setting: A ring setting in which the stone is held by a circular band of metal.

Coronet Setting: A round claw setting with crown-like design.

Crowned Harp: Used on Irish silver as a standard mark.

Cravat Pin: The same as a tie pin.

Cross-over: A style of ring, bracelet or brooch in which the stone set decorative portions bypass and lie alongside each other.

Crown Setting: An open setting resembling a crown.

Curb Chain: A chain in which the oval flattened links are twisted so that they lie flat.

Cushion Cut: A square or rectangular shape with rounded corners. Also called "antique cut".

Cymric: A trade name used by Liberty & Co. for articles sold by them which were designed and manufactured by English firms. The name was adopted in 1899.

D

Designer: A person who designs jewelry. Occasionally they are also the makers of jewelry.

Dispose': means "patent applied for" on French or Swiss made articles.

Doublet: An assembled stone consisting of two materials, usually garnet and glass.

E

Electro-plating: The process of covering metal with a coating of another metal by using electrical current.

Enamel: A glass-like material used in powder or flux form and fired on to metal.

Engine-turning: Decoration with engraved lines produced on a special lathe.

Engraving: A technique by which a design is put into a metal surface using incised lines.

F

Filigree: Ornamental designs made by using plain, twisted or plaited wire.

Findings: Mass-produced parts used to attach jewelry to the clothing or on to a person.

Fitting: Findings that are custom made for the piece of jewelry.

Foil: A thin layer or coating used on the back of stones to improve their color and brilliance.

French Jet: It is neither French nor Jet, instead this term usually refers to black glass.

G

Gate: The channel in a mold through which the molten metal flows during the white metal spin-casting process. Also refers to that part of the cast piece that is wasted.

Girdle: The polished or unpolished area between the crown and pavilion of a stone.

Gunmetal: An alloy of 90% copper and 10% tin that was very popular in the 1890's.

Gutta-percha: A hard rubber material made from the sap of a Malayan tree. Discovered in the 1840's, it was used for making jewelry, statuary and even furniture.

Gypsy Setting: A type of setting in which the stone is set down flush in the mounting.

H

Hallmark: A group of markings used on silver or gold in England since 1300 to designate the fineness of the metal, the town in which it was assayed, and the name of the maker.

Head: The fitting or finding that holds a stone.

Heft: The feel of the weight of a piece caused by its specific gravity.

Hunting Case: A watch that has a lid covering the face. A case spring is activated by pushing on the crown causing the lid to pop open.

J

Jabot Pin: A type of stick pin worn on the front of ladies blouses.

Jet: A very light weight black or brownish black material which is a variety of the coal family.

K

Karat: Pure gold is 24 karats. The karat of gold alloy is determined by the percentage of pure gold. For instance 18K gold is 750 parts pure gold and 250 parts other metal.

L

Lava Jewelry: Jewelry made of the lava from Mt. Vesuvius. Usually carved into cameos or intaglios and sold as souvenirs of the "grand tour."

Laveliere: A light scale necklace usually consisting of a pendant or pendants suspended from a chain. In the 1890-1910 era it usually had a baroque pearl appendage. The word is probably derived from the Duchess de la Valliere, a mistress of Louis XIV.

Lead Glass: Glass with a large amount of lead oxide which is used to imitate gemstones.

Line Bracelet: A flexible bracelet composed of stones of one size or graduating in size, set in a single line.

M

Macle: A flat bottomed diamond crystal.

Marcasite: A misnomer that is now a commonly accepted trade name for pyrite. Popular from the 18th century onwards.

Marquise: A boat shaped cut used for diamonds and other gem stones. Also called a "navette" shape.

Millegrain: A setting in which the metal holding the stone is composed of tiny grains or beads.

Mosaic: A piece of jewelry in which the pattern is formed by the inlaying of various colored stones or glass. Three types of mosaic work are Roman, Florentine and Venetian.

N

Necklace Lengths: Choker - 15 inches, Princess - 18 inches, Matinee - 22 inches, Opera - 30 inches, Rope - 60 inches long.

Nickel Silver: A combination of copper, nickel, zinc and sometimes small amounts of tin, lead or other metals. Also referred to as German silver.

O

Old Mine Cut: An old style of cutting a diamond in which the girdle outline is squarish, the crown is high and the table is small. It has 32 crown facets plus a table, and 24 pavilion facets plus a cutlet.

P

Paste Jewelry: Jewelry which is set with glass imitation gems. Very popular in the 18th century, it provides us with many good examples of the jewelry from that time period.

Pave Setting: A style of setting in which the stones are set as close together as possible, presenting a cobblestone effect.

Pendeloque: A faceted drop shaped stone similar to a briolette except that it has a table.

Pietra-dura: (Hard Stone). Flat slices of chalcedony, agate, jasper and lapis lazuli used in Florentine mosaic jewelry.

Pinchbeck: An alloy of copper and zinc invented by Christopher Pinchbeck in the 1720s that looked like gold. It was used for making jewelry, watches and accessories. This term is very misused today. Some English dealers refer to any piece that is not gold as "pinchbeck".

Platinum: A rare, heavy, silvery white metallic element which is alloyed with other metals and used to make fine pieces of jewelry.

Poincon: A french term for the mark on French jewelry similar to the English Hallmark.

Prongs: The wire structures that hold the stone securely in the head.

R

Repousse Work: A decorative technique of raising a pattern on metal by beating, punching or hammering from the reverse side. Often called embossing.

Rhinestone: Originally rock crystal found along the banks of the Rhine river. Today, a misnomer for colorless glass used in costume jewelry.

Rhodium: A white metallic element that is part of the platinum group. Because of its hard reflective finish it is often used as a plating for jewelry.

Riviere: A style of necklace containing individually set stones of the same size or graduating in size that are set in a row without any other ornamentations.

Rose Cut: A cutting style in which there are 24 triangular facets meeting at the top with a point. The base is always flat. Diamonds cut this way are usually cut from macles.

S

Sautoir: A long neck chain that extended beyond a woman's waist. Usually terminating in a pendant or tassel.

Jewelry Detective Supplies Order Form

10k-14k-18k *(as shown)*
Acid Testing Kit
$45.00
Quantity _____

Silver Testing Solution **$4.00**
Quantity _____

Platinum Testing Solution **$9.00**
Quantity _____

Hot Point
$22.00
Quantity _____

10X Loupe
$36.00
Quantity _____

Diamond Tester
$139.00
Quantity _____

Cup Loupe
$6.00
Quantity _____

Diamond Weight Estimator **$6.00**
Quantity _____

Pocket Size Gemstone Weight Scale **$100.00**
Quantity _____

Notching File $3.00
(not pictured)
Quantity _____

Books:

Answers to Questions About Old Jewelry, (1840-1950), C. Jeanenne Bell, $24.95
Quantity _____

Gemstones of the World, by Walter Schuman, $24.95
Quantity _____

Pocket Size Hallmark Book, $10.00
Quantity _____

Fill this form out completely and mail to:

A.D. Supplies & Tools
7325 Quivira Rd. #238
Shawnee, Kansas 66216
Telephone: (913) 962-0085

OR

Fill this form out completely and fax to:
1-800-515-3289

OR

If you prefer to call in your order, dial toll-free: **1-800-516-8356**
(Orders Only)

Sub-total $_____

Ship to: _____
_____
_____
_____

Allow 1-2 weeks for delivery.

Check, Money Order, MasterCard or Visa Credit Card Information:

MC/Visa # _____
Exp. Date _____
Name as on Credit Card:
_____

Signature: _____